MUD ON MY DOORSTEP

Reminiscences of a Yorkshire Farmwife

by

Irene Megginson

HUTTON PRESS

1987

Published by the Hutton Press Ltd.
130 Canada Drive, Cherry Burton, Beverley
East Yorkshire HU17 7SB

Copyright © 1987

Printed by Clifford Ward & Co.
(Bridlington) Ltd.
55 West Street, Bridlington
East Yorkshire YO15 3DZ

ISBN 0 907033 49 0

INTRODUCTION

The idea of writing about my early years as a "farmwife" — yes, you were married to the farm as well as to the farmer — simmered in my mind for some time until it finally boiled over two years ago, aided by a good memory and brief diaries kept since 1940. I also felt that a short account of my early years would serve as an introduction to the contrast in life-style that was to follow.

I am a great believer in the importance of recording for posterity a way of life which seems unbelievable in this age. When I have given the occasional talk on those early years as a farmer's wife, the younger generation has been amazed and obviously has found the events hard to believe.

Yet it all happened, just as I have written. One just accepted the difficulties, made the most of the good times, and was grateful for a hard-working, yet understanding husband, with a shared sense of humour — not forgetting the family of four who made it all worthwhile.

IRENE MEGGINSON
Bishop Wilton
June 1987

To Jack, with Love

TIME REMEMBERED

A "townee" born to a pampered life,
A city-style was all I knew.
'Twas a shock to become a farmer's wife —
A tough existence with much to do.

Loo down garden — no time for reading!
Lamp-light by which I could scarcely see;
Farm lads needing constant feeding —
With beef, bacon and pies for tea.

Cooking was dicey, the range made me mad;
And many a time I thought I would die
Of shame when puddings turned out sad
Or spongey cakes were far too dry.

On washday morns, for strength I'd pray,
As with "dolly" or "posher" I'd struggle and sigh,
"I'll never get washed and ironed today!" —
Bent over copper with steam rising high.

As babies came (no pills to stop 'em),
With piles of nappies, always wet,
No wonder I tried in vain to pot 'em —
Plastic pants not invented yet.

Now gadgets for this and that you'll see
In farming kitchens beyond all dreams,
But very urban, you'll all agree,
For farmers' wives are "townees" it seems!

(Written for East Yorkshire Federation
of Women's Institutes Poetry Competition 1985)

4

CHAPTER ONE

Hull in the twenties and early thirties wasn't exactly an ideal preparation for a farming life, but it offered me a happy childhood in which I soon discovered how much I enjoyed the countryside. Father ran a Fish, Game and Poultry shop. I use capital letters as all were important in his eyes, as he had worked hard to achieve ownership, and took great pride in his clean premises, with the goods displayed artistically on the street frontage.

The fish, which included all the luxuries like salmon, halibut and dover sole, rested in great blocks of ice, interspersed with colourful crabs, lobsters and prawns. Hanging in clusters from steel hooks was poultry of all kinds, with game according to the season. I remember the hares with their heads in little buckets, and the colourful plumage of pheasants, guinea fowl, and the rare capercailzie.

He loved to visit farmers and gamekeepers, and just before my memories begin he had stables for a cart mare (Daisy) as a rulley was needed for the dock journeys, and a trap pony (Nigger) for deliveries to the outer suburbs. I can only remember the motor-lorry and the van, plus whistling errand boys who delivered to our door on bicycles which sported huge wicker baskets and had the shop name on a sign fixed to the crossbar.

A spell of good trade led to a move from a Victorian house in Dover Street, off Spring Bank, to the "posh" surroundings of Newland Park, where we quickly settled down in a large bungalow of New Zealand design with an open verandah along two sides.

There was a spacious garden, not all formal thank goodness, as the area under and around a huge old willow was a haven for the gang of tree climbing friends I seemed to accumulate. We had strong ropes, one with a tyre attached, and loved to climb up to a stout, gnarled branch where, after carefully edging our way astride (hard on knickers!) we waited for someone at ground level to swing up the rope which conveniently curled itself around the branch. Tarzan-like we would hang on while carefully balancing to get a foothold before launching blissfully into space. We loved the tyre-rope too, with one of us sitting inside and another standing on top. If an adult happened to be around they would oblige by setting us off in a sick-making circular flight!

The author with her mother outside "Oimara," their bungalow in Newland Park, Hull. The house was "blitzed" during the Second World War.

If it all got too exhausting there was always the old ship's hammock slung between two nearby trees. No wonder no grass managed to grow in this play area. Old friends, even now, when reminiscing still say of Newland Park days: "Do you remember the willow tree, and the ropes?"

My mother decided to make use of the wilder part of the garden to rear poultry and produce eggs for the shop. Up-to-date hen houses were built and wire netted runs made. Leghorns, Wyandottes, plus some strange, exotic tufted birds — I think they were known as Houdans — were soon strutting, pecking, scratching or cackling in their enclosures. They were fed with maize, and when I see sweetcorn on menus today I feel inclined to mutter "chicken food"! I liked to watch them jumping up and down to taste the delights of surplus cabbages or other greens hung up on strings from the wire netting.

An open drain ran along one side of the garden — Hull had numerous drains in those days — and we even had a small rowing boat. It was quite an adventure to pass under Cottingham Road, opposite what is now the University, carefully lying back in the boat while propelling ourselves along with our hands on the roof of the low bridge. I wasn't allowed to take the boat on my own, but older sisters with their boyfriends had fun in it.

There was a little offshoot of the drain wired off and rather grandly called "the ravine." Here were ducks, which amused us "uptails all." Once they escaped through the front garden hedge, and solemnly made a procession along the pavement.

I expect we were considered rather an odd family to settle in this suburban "Park." We even kept turkeys — I never cared for their "gobbling" — and later on we had two nanny goats in an adjoining paddock with frontage on Cottingham Road. This was the last field to be built on, and a neighbour kept a pony in it. I was sometimes given a ride, which was a great treat. With dogs, cats and rabbits around too I was well used to animals at this stage.

Our household differed from the neighbours in not having a maid in uniform, which was then the normal thing. Instead we had Lill, who came to us, before I was born, as a "char" in Dover Street and eventually was asked to live in, becoming cook, housemaid and nanny, while still tackling the charring jobs! Lill had a great capacity for work. In my infancy she coped with a difficult, squawling baby who demanded gripe-water throughout the night and fed me with unsuitable things — "Anything to get a bit of peace."

Later she needed "eyes in the back of my head" to deal with my mischievous tricks. At one stage I was collected by one of her relations on wash-days and taken across Hull by tram to be amused for the day and kept out of the way of all the hard work!

It was Lill who milked the goats. I don't think we used the milk as it wasn't popular, but we had a few customers who collected it for invalids. Lill also liked to fit in some gardening jobs, although we had a part-time gardener. At an early age I was interested in flowers, and I still think of lupins, delphiniums, the deep purple campanulas and red-hot pokers as "Newland Park flowers."

Mother was proud of her sweetpeas, and had special scissors for cutting them which held the stalk of the cut bloom upright till transferred to the shallow basket. I wish I could find such scissors now! The flowers (several heads to each stalk) were always arranged in a silver-plated epergne with gypsophila to add to the elegant effect, and placed in the centre of the mahogany dining table.

I often visited a large house across the road of the "nouveau riche" type, where there was a little boy of my age who became a well-loved playmate. I'm told he once remarked: "When I grow up,

Irene, I shall marry you!" to which I replied: "Oh, but Kenny, you'll have to grow up and earn lots and lots of money first!" I probably felt I should like a house like "Eastfield," with all the latest furnishings and decorations. I can still see that vast drawing room, richly carpeted, and with curtains of pink velour stretching across the big bay — which incidentally made a lovely stage for our "concerts." The three-piece suite was covered in pink brocade and adorned with antimacassars of black satin, fringed in silver!

Little Kenny had expensive toys, a beautiful fort with hundreds of lead soldiers, and a little tin gramophone which played tiny records. I only recall my favourite "Turkey in the Straw," which was a very lively tune. Kenny drove a smart little pedal car, with a B.P. petrol can on the running board, while I galloped round the garden paths astride an old broom with reins attached — this was my pony!

The loo in this house was the most impressive I have ever seen, even to this day. In fact, when I was first shown where to "go" I closed the door and stood there quite bewildered. A huge easy chair with a cane seat, back and arms confronted me, and only the chain dangling overhead convinced me that this was it!

Carefully I lifted the smart cane seat and, sure enough, there was the familiar lavatory bowl with wooden surround. Obviously this family went in for comfort for all occasions. Incidentally, it was my friendship with Kenny which educated me in the fact that little boys didn't need to sit down on the toilet but had a handy device which saved taking one's pants down!

This family had a real maid in black and white uniform, also a "car" and a full-time gardener. The garden was immaculate, with tennis court, summer house, terrace, loggia, and a circular lawn for clock golf. Somehow though, both house and garden lacked our carefree atmosphere, and there were no pets at all.

Our first car was a black "Saxon" with folding hood and mica windows, driven by my oldest sister, who was very tiny and could hardly see above the big steering wheel. The car was the means of widening our horizons, as holidays were scarce because the shop could not be left.

We had excursions to the Moors and to the sea, winding our way slowly through quiet lanes and learning to love the Wold villages on the "scenic" route to Scarborough. We always avoided main roads, and often picnicked in gravel pits, loving the wild flowers and watching lambs in the fields. In Holderness my father liked to call on

8

farmers or keepers he knew, and we explored Kilnsea, Spurn Point and Hornsea.

It was during Newland Park days that I was taken to the theatre for the first time — a never-to-be-forgotten occasion which was the start of a lifelong interest in play-going.

On this occasion my parents took me to see "Peter Pan" at the old Alexandra Theatre, which was, I think, in Carr Lane. "Peter Pan" had been the first long book which I had been able to read through by myself, and I can remember almost devouring it, so much was my imagination stirred by this story. Sitting in the dress circle, clutching my mother's opera glasses, I was completely absorbed as the action-packed play unfolded before me. I still think Peter's entrance through the open window of the Darlings' nursery is one of the great moments of the theatre, and to a small child whose delight was merely swinging on ropes, the sight of a mortal actually flying was almost too much for me — especially when this part was played by the very famous actress Jean Forbes-Robertson!

Glued to my seat I fixed the glasses on her face to bring the expressions, so realistically registered, almost within touching distance. This was even more dramatic in the "underground" scene when Tinkerbell was dying. How I clapped to restore that rather tiresome fairy to life!

Today Barrie is dismissed as a sentimental writer with a very odd private life, but I still feel addicted to the charm of "Peter Pan," and have seen the play since in Hull with our children, and in Leeds with grandchildren. Someday, who knows, I may even take great-grand-children.

Another theatre memory of those days was being taken by Lill to a Grand Theatre pantomime. I can only recall the novelty of the journey as we took a strange "taxi," which was a glorified motorbike with sidecar!

CHAPTER TWO

Alas, this era only lasted five years. I believe the business suffered through an unscrupulous partner, and we reluctantly left Newland Park to move to an Edwardian villa in the Avenues. "Grown-up" affairs were seldom discussed with children in those days.

This house was semi-detached and quite spacious, in the typical style of the period. My mother had it completely redecorated in the latest fashion. Elaborate floral paper was "panelled" on a plain background and outlined with borders. All the rooms were wall-papered in this fussy manner, and I can still see the exotic birds perched in palm trees which seemed very pretty after the plain pastel walls of the Newland Park home.

My bedroom, at the back of the house, was over the scullery, and was somewhat unique in having had a small lift installed by the previous owners. They had a young family, and a nursemaid. Meals had been served in the nursery, hence this little service lift with two shelves. I thought it great fun, and plagued Lill to put my breakfast in it on non-school mornings! When having friends to tea we would send notes down with requests for what we fancied, and this meal would be eaten at a small table with matching chairs set out in the bay window.

We knew little of neighbours in the Avenues, but a family opposite called Johnson became well-known when their daughter Amy made her famous solo flight to Australia which resulted in world-wide fame. We all listened with intent interest to wireless news as she valiantly flew on with numerous setbacks and adventures. My mother read aloud from the latest newspaper editions so we could all hear the recent reports at the same moment, and we listened, hanging on to every word.

On the day of her return to Hull with a civic reception, watched by thousands of enthusiastic admirers, we were amused to see the front garden of the family house suddenly burst into bloom as geraniums and calceolarias were delivered in pots and hurriedly planted! We had invited various friends to make use of our front bedroom windows as a viewing point, and we waited up there excitedly as the cheering crowds lining the road gave advance warning of the arrival of the open car with "our Amy" perched up on the back seat, wearing a navy dress with red and white striped scarf. We cheered and waved little flags as she left the limelight to join her quiet, reserved parents in their home. Hull was indeed proud of that brave young girl.

I must have missed the space, the animals, and the tree at our Newland Park home, but like most nine-year-olds I quickly adapted, while my parents and Lill must have felt devastated. I had a large swing and rings at the bottom of the narrow garden, and we still had the two dogs, but best of all I was nearer to Pam, Jill, Betty and Maureen, as well as the convent school to which we walked. Before that I had taken a tram, or ridden my little bike. The traffic in Cottingham Road, Newland, and Princes Avenue, was then quite safe for a child, though I nearly fell one day when a wheel caught in the tram lines.

We were always interested in identifying the trees which lined the Avenues, and in people's gardens. Even their curtains were discussed, and all the different styles of architecture. I have always felt grateful for the "convent" years, as the friends I made as a small child have remained close, and even today one may regain contact with one who had appeared to have been lost — yet the bond of those early years together is still strong. Perhaps having small classes of a dozen or so helped.

I spent much "out of school time" with Jill, whose father was a doctor. The house was large and double-fronted. There was a family of three, and on the attic floor was the boys' bedroom and big playroom. On the lower floor was a sitting room — which seemed strange to me — and a wide landing where we practised hand-stands against the doors (first removing our shoes), or standing on our heads. At that time the staff consisted of a young cook and housemaid, and this craze spread to them, as we discovered after hearing strange thumping coming from the kitchen one evening! I have an idea they would be asked to stop such high jinks.

The surgery was downstairs, and another room doubled for family meals and as a waiting room where we caught glimpses of a row of "panel" patients. Doctors in those days visited private patients in their homes, even for trivial complaints. I was fascinated by a brass speaking tube set in the wall near the front door. This connected to the doctor's bedroom for night calls, as telephones were not commonplace in the early thirties.

The family was rather "higher class" than mine, and when there I

11

learned to appreciate china tea, croutons in soup, and to sprinkle fine crisp crumbs on the bread sauce!

We still saw working horses on the streets, and I remember the "crossing sweeper" who gathered up the horse dung in a push cart. There was also a dear little old lady in Edwardian-style black bonnet, cape and dress. She turned the handle of a barrel organ which produced toe-tapping melodies and made us develop sprightly skipping steps as we made our way into Pearson's Park, where an aviary and parrot house proved an amusement, if only for the raucous shrieks which resounded round the high dome glass building.

About this time the firms who made ice-cream began the novel idea of sending out men on tricycles with a deep white box in front of the handlebars. This container was full of mouthwatering ice-creams such as twopenny blocks, penny water-ices or "choc bars." Walls and Eldorado must have been keen rivals, and they supplied customers with cardboard letter E's or W's to place in front-room windows to ask them to call. I think both varieties were equally delicious as we made use of both cards.

The convent was a cold school in winter, and we hugged the radiators in our "recreation" period, and suffered from chilblains. We wore a somewhat outlandish uniform of a black sateen long-sleeved overall on top of our white blouses, and navy box-pleated tunics. Over this garment we wore a long sash, which varied in colour according to which form one belonged, and which wound round the waist, crossed at the back, then slotted through shoulder loops and finally tied in a bow at the back!

When taken off, the overalls were hung in the draughty cloakroom and the sashes neatly rolled up to straighten any creases. Our tunics kept very clean, as they only saw the light of day in gym lessons or when playing games. They had box pleats from a yoke, and these tended to fan out in an embarrassing fashion as busts developed. When performing exercises, which involved turning upside-down, we had bands of narrow elastic which would be pulled down from the waists to the hem of our tunics to save such indecent sights as a pair of navy-blue woolly knickers!

We had an up-to-date lab, and a "studio" for art, and most subjects were well taught by qualified mistresses wearing their gowns at all times — some faded into rusty black — and mortar boards for special occasions. Some of the nuns also taught various

12

lessons, but unfortunately I had a mental block about mathematics which was a compulsory subject for Senior Oxford or Matriculation, which were the equivalent of modern "A" and "O" Levels. There were some boarders who must have found life rather grim with no "common room." The dormitories were on the third floor, and the beds were separated by white curtains.

I loved elocution, which was an "extra" and gave me parts in plays. For years I enjoyed dancing lessons, often going three times a week. The evening classes meant a lone walk through side streets, and in winter it was dark except for gas lamps, yet no-one thought I was "at risk," as our cities seemed safer in those days. The lamps were lit by lamplighters who walked the streets at dusk, igniting each street light by pushing their long poles through the base of each glass to turn on the gas.

No-one thought of wearing anything more glamorous than a summer dress for dancing classes, and the only extras we needed were ballet shoes, or steel plates added to our ankle straps for "tap." Now, even tiny tot pupils wear leotards and head-bands and look like miniature members of a professional ballet company. We did, however, have pretty dresses for displays which we gave at dances in the winter or at garden parties in the summer. These were made at low cost by a dressmaker who slaved away in the living room of her house in a street off Anlaby Road. The entire wall space was taken up by tarlatan frilled fairy frocks suspended from the picture rail.

"Tommy Foster," who ran the dancing school, was a great character. He must have been middle-aged then, as he seemed old to me. Rather plump, but very light on his feet, he demonstrated the art of ballet and tap-dancing, but it was for "ballroom" that his classes were famous, with evening sessions for adults on Saturday nights. The hall where we danced was long and rather narrow, with two coal fires in winter. The pianist, Miss Foster, was a relative, and a young man called Bertie was, I think, a nephew. He helped on the instruction side.

We used the trams a lot of course. Halfpenny rides till fourteen, so if small in stature as I was, one could get by with a "ha'penny" till sixteen. We were all keen about going to the pictures, and the stars of those films were our idols. On Saturday afternoons it cost seven old pence for a cinema seat, and usually we had "tuppence" for a Mars Bar or Crunchie to munch while gazing entranced at activities on the screen.

During our weekend drives along the coast in the year when I was fourteen, we discovered the little village of Fraisthorpe within two miles of a very quiet and peaceful beach. Few cars found their way down the narrow lane with cornfields on either side, and there was plenty of parking space near the sand dunes. Even my parents took to bathing costumes which in the old snapshots looked quite disgusting! Made of thin, clinging material, they stuck to one's body when wet, and the result was revealing and rather indecent!

However, a good time was had by all, and complete with striped tent and deck chairs on the smooth, golden sand we were reluctant to leave this pleasant place to return to Hull. There was an old cottage, partly demolished, which stood near the edge of the dunes and belonged to Auburn Farm, the last remaining house of the old village, long lost to the ever-eroding relentless sea. It was said that the church had disappeared centuries ago and the coastal road had once passed that way.

In our day, teas were served from the ruined cottage by the family from the nearby farm. Like many other farmers between the wars, they were finding these bad years financially, and any opportunity to make a little profit was seized upon.

One Saturday evening my parents decided to call at Manor House, a square, red brick farmhouse in the village, to see if there was any chance of finding accommodation, and so save the drive back to Hull, only to motor out again on Sunday morning. Such an odd chance decision led to a lifelong association with the Megginson family!

This particular branch, at Duggleby, of a widespread family had come down from the large high Wold farm to try to recover financial losses on this smaller lowland venture. They were keen to get in the "summer visitor" trade, and we were welcomed as the very first paying guests. It was a blissful world to me with cows, sheep and carthorses. Before long I was even riding a horse, the hunter belonging to the Megginsons' son Jack, and jogging round the paddock with great confidence, but I soon hit the ground! "Darkie" could also be driven in a trap — in fact there were so many delights on the farm that the beach seemed dull in comparison.

So, for that school holiday I was left during the week to "live as family" in the kitchen. I rode a carthorse in a wagon when leading corn, and learned to recognise the difference between oats, wheat and barley, and also between hay and straw! I also had to get

14

Farmer Harold Megginson (Jack's father) competing in the driving trials organised by Mark Sykes at Duggleby in 1916.

Summer visitors help with the harvest.

accustomed to broad Yorkshire words live "shav" for sheaf, and "wots" for oats, to say nothing of "yow" for ewe!

I loved to help prepare cattle food in the old "grainary," which smelt so delicious, with fragrant odours, rising from stacked slabs of cotton and linseed cake. These had to be put through the cake-crusher as needed, and turning that big iron wheel (at least it seemed big to me) with the wooden handle was a job I could tackle — in short spells.

There were great heaps of golden grain and piles of "Fox's sacks." Jack gave me many exciting rides on the sack barrow, running quickly over the boarded floor to make hair-raising one-wheeled turns at the corners!

I got on very well with Jack (who seemed quite old at twenty-one!) and his sisters, and returned for a short time in the Christmas holidays. There was no bathroom in the farmhouse: a large zinc bath was filled with hot water on Saturdays, and bathing took place in the kitchen with a discreet watch kept on the door! There were two "little houses" down the front garden path. One had a single seat, and the other two. There were well scrubbed out, whitewashed walls, and from a nail dangled neatly cut squares of newspaper! But — not the place to linger — and if one tried to read, the squares never matched up!

Teenagers were immature in the thirties, and during other holiday times we still climbed trees when in the country, and loved to ride on the running board of our car, a Vauxhall saloon which my mother learned to drive when my sister married. She was a brave driver and tackled bumpy by-roads, often with gates. My friend, Pam, and I would cling to the frames of the open windows with hair blowing in the breeze, thinking it all great fun as we jumped off the car to open and shut the gates, sometimes shooing stock away first.

We picked cowslips on the banks of the railway line in Kipling-coates and sat on the rails to watch the trains. Lill, of course, was with us, and provided lovely picnics. We always boiled a tin kettle on a little spirit stove. I have never learned to make such delicious, thin sandwiches, or perhaps the bread was better in those days, and schoolgirl appetites more keen.

Once, when ascending Staxton Hill after a trip to Scarborough, we had a heavier load than usual with extra friends of the family. The car suddenly stopped chugging, and gradually came to a halt. In fact, it didn't halt, but began running backwards! Mother gave orders to get out and find a large stone to put under a wheel. This we did with great speed, only too glad to disembark. That stone saved the day.

With lighter load the car went into action again, and when the summit was reached Mother waited for us as, puffing and excited by our adventure, we took our seats and continued on our way back to Hull.

Going through Beverley Westwood one evening a tyre burst, and after skidding the car turned over. We were shaken, slightly bruised, but otherwise unhurt. Afterwards I could only remember the sight of Lill's bloomers above my head! Someone must have helped push the car upright again and change the wheel, as we continued our journey. It was one time when none of my friends was with us.

Another little holiday adventure occurred when my friend Betty was staying with us. Betty had been one of the "tree" gang, but left the convent when her family moved to Essex. My brother-in-law had a laundry business with a branch in Scarborough, so it seemed a good chance for Betty and I to have a day by the sea, as our car had had to be sold after the death of my father.

Brother-in-law dropped us in the centre of the town and arranged to pick us up in the same place at six o'clock that evening. We had a happy day, swimming and enjoying the sun, and promptly turned up at the meeting place. No brother-in-law! We waited an hour before deciding (quite rightly as it happened) that he had forgotten us. What should we do? Betty suggested the police station, as we'd always been told: "If in trouble find a policeman!"

We asked a chap on point duty how to get to the station and walked in feeling far from confident. The staff there were very helpful after taking all the details. In fact, the sergeant showed much more interest on hearing Betty's address in Braintree, Essesx. "My old Dad came from there!" and we were well in favour! They let us use the phone to talk to Mother in Hull, and told her we would be taken to lodgings if she would pay the bill the following day. A meeting was arranged at the said address on the following afternoon as brother-in-law (yes, he had forgotten us till back in Hull) could not get there any earlier.

We were then told to "follow me," and a kindly P.C. took us through the town to find "Mrs. Jeffries" who would look after us. It was dusk by this time, but we found ourselves being escorted into quite a large hall where a pleasant woman greeted us. We were shown up many stairs to a high attic room and left to settle down in a comfortable bed. No sponge bags, no nightgowns, but it was all rather fun when we were no longer worried.

We woke early, rushed to our bedroom window, and gasped! We were actually in a smart hotel (Jeffreyville) high on the North Cliff, with a wonderful view across the bay! What an adventure! Hotels were quite out of our experience. We felt very untidy in our crumpled cotton frocks, bare legs, and dusty sandals. I cannot remember much about breakfast, but we were soon out in the town again. We couldn't waste this bonus day, so we walked all the way to the South Bay swimming pool. I do remember having a very sore toe where a sandal strap rubbed it! We had less than a shilling between us, but preferred swimming tickets to food. Checking up on this with Betty she says we shared a Mars Bar!

Anyway, we had a lovely swim and then trudged back to Jeffreyville where we met brother-in-law, who paid our bill and drove us home. This all appealed to our sense of adventure, and we talked about it for months afterwards.

CHAPTER THREE

On leaving school at sixteen there was the problem of what to do. I was still stage-struck, and with my friend Mickey had seen all the plays at Hull Rep and idolised the company of very good actors and actresses. Mickey went to live in London and on to Drama School, but it wasn't a suitable career for me, or should I say I wasn't suitable for the career!

I filled in a year with art lessons, took elocution exams, and generally "messed about." After my father's death, Mother had valiantly taken over the management of the shop. Gradually she pulled it out of money difficulties and stayed at the helm till well in her seventies. Things were rather difficult in 1937, and we had moved to a smaller house in the Avenues, where I had brand new furniture in the little back bedroom. The dressing table, wardrobe and two-drawer chest cost five pounds and a bedside table twelve shillings and sixpence. Lill went with me to a side-street store to choose them and Mother thought them poor quality, but they lasted well into my married life, and the little table is still in use.

I still attended some dancing classes, having learned a lot with that Tommy Foster. I went on to Miss Pocock (rather refined) and then tried Madame Sharrah (another character!) when I heard of auditions for the chorus needed for the Repertory Company's Christmas production of "Alice in Wonderland." I made the chorus! Amateur and unpaid, but for three weeks I felt part of that lively production and loved every minute of it!

Many people in that cast went on to be well-known on the stage and on T.V., the most famous being Jimmy Stewart, who played Humpty Dumpty. Later he changed his name to Stewart Grainger to avoid confusion with the already well-known James Stewart.

In 1980 I read his autobiography and decided to send an old photograph of "Alice" — the whole cast — and much to my delight he wrote a sweet letter which began "Dear Irene," and ended "Love Jimmy." What a feather in my cap — but would you believe it, the grandchildren all said "But who is Stewart Grainger?"

However, something had to be decided on, and as horses were another interest in my life — though I'd only had comparatively few ridings lessons — it was arranged that I should join my friend Joan in Devon. Joan had decided to train as a girl groom in spite of having done well in matriculation exams, and her parents had been down to see a riding school attached to a farm guest house on the edge of Dartmoor.

Like many such establishments, even today, our labour was the slave type, and our work was only endured because we loved the horses and ponies so much. I seem to remember the sum of one hundred pounds for the six months training, then we could "earn our keep" for another six months! On the top of this, we had to buy expensive breeches, with ankle boots and leggings (leather), two tweed jackets, a hunting jacket and three khaki overalls which had to be worn for all stable work.

We were cooked for, our boots were cleaned daily by the odd-job man, and our bedrooms cleaned, but there seemed to be strict rules about almost everything we did.

The proprietor was a tough, horsey spinster with a tongue like a whiplash, and a voice like a corncrake when angered. Her knowledge of horse ailments and stable routine was excellent, but the riding tuition was almost non-existent, especially compared with post-war standards of equitation.

The farmhouse was picturesque and the thatched roof was a novelty to us Northerners. The views all round were incredibly beautiful, and we learned to love the cleave, the woodlands and, of course, the nearby Moor. In all weathers we exercised around the deep, tunnel-like lanes, and when not miserably holding our heads down to avoid the constant battering from unrelenting wind and rain, we could feast our townee eyes on the profusion of wild flowers on the banks. During those early weeks the fine penetrating rain seemed to soak our clothes every day in spite of thick riding macs (another costly garment) and brown felt hats, the stain from which dripped on our collars!

I remember silently quoting bits of appropriate poetry during these rides. "The rain it raineth every day..." or "Along the dripping leafless woods the stirrup touching either shoe, she rode astride as troopers do!" W. Morris certainly described my feelings only too well.

As the countryside became a delight in all shades of fresh spring green and new shoots of bracken appeared in the rock crevasses of the Moors, life took on a new outlook. In spite of our restricted life, or perhaps because of it, the rides over the Moor became times of great joy.

The characters of our sure-footed ponies (horses were less reliable on the rough terrain of boulders and steep rocky tracks) caused us to love them and treat them as people rather than animals. The wild ponies with foals at foot delighted us, and the little villages, the stone buildings, the rugged tors, and the rushing streams are still fresh in my memory.

Visits to the blacksmith's shop in Widdecombe could be quite a worry, with all the tourist display of "Uncle Tom Cobley" china and souvenirs stacked around the entrance to this famous forge. A skittish pony could so easily have sent a shelf-full shattering to the ground!

The farmhouse, yes there were pigs there, and calves tended by a lad, and of course a cow for milk and cream, was very isolated. No public transport came within reach of us, but once a month we were permitted to go out for a day, paying half-a-crown for the seat in a car belonging to a neighbouring farm, which was the unofficial taxi service!

If you only go out once a month it's amazing how much more you enjoy yourself than if this privilege was a weekly occurrence! Two girls usually went together. At first there were a few students, and we really indulged ourselves.

After shopping at Newton Abbot, we gorged ourselves over lunch and cream cakes from a pastry shop called Madge Mellor's. We usually saw a film before meeting our taxi-driver, and occasionally took a bus for a short visit to Torquay.

In the evenings we played games — Monopoly was new then — or wrote letters. No radio to liven things up, and bed-time all the year round was nine o'clock! If we wanted to read in bed we had to use candles as the electricity generator was expensive. On fine, light evenings we loved to walk across the Big Meadow (all of nine acres!) to the cleave, or up the winding lane to the village of Manaton.

We did have half a day off on Sunday, either church in the morning or a walk in the afternoon!

It was my first experience of living away from home, and the discipline was good I'm sure, and an excellent preparation for life as a farmer's wife!

In the summer we had "paying guests" all over the house, stables, and garden. We got much less riding then with all the tack-cleaning and waiting for the "Ride" to return so we could take away the sweaty horses to be cleaned and fed.

In winter we had the added excitement and interest of hunting days. We met other people, and saw far more of the countryside, either on woodland or moorland days. It was a friendly Hunt, and not too smart. I was noted for falling off when galloping downhill, but there was always someone ready and willing to catch my mount, and help me up again!

I stayed for eighteen months altogether. Joan went back to Yorkshire, but I had another friend there, Margery, who later also married a farmer, and she and her husband both became life-long friends.

A "groom" job at ten shillings per week "plus keep" followed this training, and I was lucky to be with a most interesting "county" family near Totnes. Again it was hard work, but less isolated, and I was taken around by the family, even rising to the dizzy heights of a ball at Admiralty House, Devonport!

Poor Lill hurriedly made a black velvet cloak for this occasion (it lasted for many years, and ended by being used in countless school plays) and posted off my one evening dress, blue watered silk with puffed sleeves.

I returned home in the summer of 1939 while the family went to Scotland for the salmon fishing, and read a report in the local paper of a gymkhana in Driffield where Jack Megginson had won a prize!

Joan happened to be at home then, and could drive a car (why didn't I learn then?) so we set off to Fraisthorpe and surprised the Megginson family. That, one might say, was the beginning of the end, as far as my future was concerned!

CHAPTER FOUR

I spent much of that holiday helping on the farm again, and was there when war was declared. Not knowing what impact war would make to this "green and pleasant land," my mother felt worried about my returning to far-off Devon. So, my job there came to an end, and my trunk was sent up by train to Yorkshire, where my "groom" clothes came in useful for my new work as unofficial Land Girl to the Megginsons. Harvest was in full swing, the sun shone daily, and it was difficult to believe we were at war.

I'd grown up a little since school holiday visits to the farm, and no longer went around asking embarrassing questions as to why tups needed "rud" on their chests (to mark the ewes when being served in case any readers are wondering) and why the big Shire stallion was brought round every three weeks!

Now I became part of the work force, taking my place in a niche on the corn stack, with my long-handled fork ready to lift each "shav" — sent up from the wagon below — to the stacker (Jack) above me. I looked forward to the arrival of the great baskets of food at "looance" time. "Looance," by the way, is a broad Yorkshire word derived from the old "allowance" which referred to the measure of beer per man.

On many big farms there was a "brew house" where beer was brewed on the premises. Jack remembers when the big stone jars of beer were taken to the field in a straw-lined crate, and two men could share a mug. One drank till he could see the bottom of the mug, then he would hand it to his partner to finish the drink.

In that sunny harvest, at the beginning of the last war, a great enamel can of tea would arrive for "looance." The men all liked their drink sweet, and a special bottle was put in the basket for me, as I couldn't bear sugary tea. We ate newly baked chocolate cakes, or great slices of "ground rice," "curd cheesecake" or "hotcakes" straight from the oven, and oozing melted butter. Often there was a hunk of cheese per person too. We drank from thick white pot mugs, pint size, and everyone enjoyed this brief relaxation from the hard work.

The last of the corn was safely in the stack before we attended the Harvest Festival in the little church of St. Edmund opposite Lodge Farm. This church was officially a "chapel of ease" and not licensed for weddings or funerals. It was a simple building with chairs for seating and a rather old harmonium, on which Jack's mother played the hymns.

For the first time I felt part of the service, as did the rest of the congregation. All of us had been actively engaged in some way with the gathering of the harvest, and all sang lustily. Afterwards we trooped across to Lodge Farm where Miss Hyde had prepared a great feast for all and sundry. It was always a joke that the vicar enjoyed the sherry trifle so much, and we were all thankful that the harvest had been "safely gathered in" though some folk insisted on adding "bar rakings" under their breath as they sang that popular hymn.

The Hyde family were good neighbours, and often during harvest the two farms worked as one and shared labour.

When "our" harvest was finished we took horses and wagons up to the beginning of the Wold land above Carnaby to give a "day's leading" to a farmer's widow who still had corn out in stooks. I shall always remember that day, as even then I loved the hills, and working in those golden fields with wide views across to the sea and Bridlington Bay sparkling in the distance gave me a wonderful feeling of being at one with the Wolds and the coast. Everyone was tired, the horses as well, when "knocking off" time came and we rumbled back home in the wide, empty wagons, thankful that we had been able to help a less fortunate friend.

The Hydes' farm, being larger than the Megginsons', employed a foreman, shepherd, wagoner, bullocky, and a couple of lads, as well as father and son. "We" had father and son, plus "wag," bullocky, and a young lad. I fitted in anywhere, a sort of "Tommy owt" as the saying was.

I learned a little hand-milking, but never became very good at this job. "Old Herbert" helped Jack to milk, and was rather an unsavoury character. With an old cloth cap on top of tousled hair, he buried his head in the flank of the cow. "Noo then 'awd Brin," he'd say to the Brindle heifer as she lifted her leg and nearly poked it in the bucket. I must say that when I did achieve a rhythmic "ping, ping" in the pail it was a rewarding effort, as I sat on a three-legged stool, rather precariously balanced near the drainage channel.

Jack taught me how to put the gearing on a carthorse, and I learned a little of the satisfying art of ploughing with the oldest and most steady pair, the sweet and gentle grey mare, Bonny, and the

25

The author pictured with "Bonny" and "Smiler" in 1937.

crafty old dark brown gelding, Tinker. It was easy to learn the commands of "Gee back" (right) and "Wharve" (left) and "Whoa" (stop) but "stringing them up" to keep a steady pace was not at all easy. The men seemed to give a quick flick of the strings and they got an instant reaction as the horses felt the impact of rope on flank. My feeble efforts had little success, and I would try to quickly pick up a clot or small stone to hurl at Tinker's massive, muscular quarters as he dawdled up the furrow.

When we eventually neared the headland, the crafty old horse was one jump ahead of me and if not shouted at and pulled back would turn too quickly, making the share jump out of the furrow, thus making a proper mess of the job! I don't think I did more than half a day's ploughing at a time, but I'm glad to have done even a little of that age-old method of working the land.

Now we have gigantic ploughs (reversible) and as many as six furrows, or the cultivating is done with a "triple K" or "power harrow." One man does more in a few hours than several lads with their two-horse teams and single furrow ploughs achieved in a long day of walking up and down for hours on end. No wonder many lads had flat feet!

There was a grand little cob called Ginger. He was also ridden —

26

Farmer's son (Jack) with a well-loved pair, "Mettle" and "Boxer" in 1937.

"Boxer" scruffling turnips.

a true "Shepherd's hack." Farmer Megginson was lame, the result of a simple accident in his young days when he fell over a sheep trough, and this made him appear older than his years. He drove round the fields with Ginger in the float, keeping an eye on the men, or taking the looances. Perhaps he had a dead sheep to bring up from the field, or nets and stakes to be taken down. It was an easy way for him to get around and to be useful at the same time. It was a sad day when Ginger died of a twisted gut, although he was a good age.

I always liked to see the carthorses, eight of them, going down to the pond for water. Large feet plodding down the drive, or in cold weather feeling skittish enough to give a squeal and a buck before breaking into a trot. They splashed about "pawting" the water, while "wag" called them up from the stable door: "Nooo then! 'Ow many mair tarmes?" as they ignored his voice. Then one would lead the way back to the warmth of their straw-filled stall, with a manger of oats and "caff" and racks stacked with good, sweet hay. Smart, Smiler, Jet and Boxer all had different characters, and needed to be treated as individuals.

Carting muck from the fold yard to the field was another job I helped with. "Plugging" muck was the name for this operation,

"Captain" and "Topper" yoked to a corn-drill.

Yoked for "dragging" after lunch – the poor things look weary after a hard morning's work.

"Robin" being broken in by Jack with long reins.

which was unpopular hard work, and smelly of course. "This is a job they'll never get machines to do," muttered Farmer Megginson, as he leaned on his fork to have a "wind." We did get a rest while sitting on the wagon sides during the journey to the field, partly along the main road which had been cut through the farm fields in the late twenties. Thus the traffic stopped going through the village, and made it much more peaceful. This strip of road was made of concrete, and the wagon wheels rumbled noisily over the slightly ridged surface.

CHAPTER FIVE

After some months of land-girl work Jack's sister became seriously ill with a long, terminal illness, and was nursed at home most of the time by her devoted mother, so I became an "indoor" help to relieve her of some of the domestic chores.

Having had my mother and Lill around during my years at home, I knew little about running a house, especially one with such a lack of "mod. cons." — amenities taken for granted by most townspeople then, and almost all country folk now.

At least there was a bathroom which, with a smart blue "Yorkist" range, had been installed during the time I was in Devonshire. The only snag was that baths were restricted, owing to the "pumping up" necessary to fill the tank. This manually operated pump in the back kitchen took twenty minutes of pushing a wooden handle to and fro before the correct water level was reached. All the same, the bath, when one got into it, was a great luxury compared with the old zinc one dragged into the kitchen and filled from the side-boiler of the black-leaded range.

The new "Yorkist" only needed a soapy cloth and a bit of Vim to keep it clean. I was taught to be thrifty by Mrs. Megginson, and one small economy was in the use of Vim. With war-time efforts in saving labour the tins came with just the pattern of holes in the top. We made holes by hitting a nail over the dots, using a small hammer. "Only punch two holes," said Mrs. Megginson, "it makes the stuff last longer!"

Near the "Yorkist" was the old "wall oven," a vast cast-iron affair let into the wall with a fire underneath shut off by a little iron door similar to that under the copper used for wash-day hot water. The big oven was wonderful for baking a large batch of "plate" pies, and seven bread loaves slipped in easily. It had three large brass knobs which were attached to rods. When pulled to and fro they cleared soot from the flues.

Actually, the modern "Yorkist" was a brute to tackle when flues needed attention. No wonder Jack's mother still wore a coarse apron over her everyday wrap-around cotton print. Coarse aprons were made of sack cloth and tied at the waist — easily undone and slipped off when answering the door!

Cleaning the flues necessitated rolling sleeves high above the elbows, as one pushed a little hand brush as far as possible through the narrow cavities after removing little metal plates. The even smaller flues were dealt with by pushing a special brush on a long flexible wire into the flues, which had to be kept free of soot to keep the draught flowing freely. The soot one hopefully collected after this dirty job could be raked out from under the oven.

Keeping these ovens at the right heat was not easy, as some days the wind was too strong, and the fire roared underneath when the damper (why damper?) was pulled out, yet on still days no amount of coaxing with special lengths, or thicknesses, of sticks could persuade the thing to heat up. Hopefully one got it very hot for pastry, then let it cool a little for putting in bread, then as the cakes baked and were taken out, the temperature was right for finishing off the loaves.

I was told there was a great skill in "setting" an oven, and not all bricklayers were good at this job. Some ovens it seemed never "drew" well, whatever the weather!

Bread-making was the first cooking job I learned. I rather enjoyed it, kneeling on the rag rug in front of the fire (or away from it in summer). I carefully mixed in the frothy yeast mixture, and loved the feeling of reaching the stage when it all went smooth and elastic, and a good kneading session followed.

We used a big earthenware bowl with yellow glazed interior. Flour was bought by the stone, and it must have been of better quality than we get today, as the loaves kept fresh between the twice weekly baking days. Always Tuesdays and Fridays. Meat and potato pie for dinner, followed by rice pudding, year in and year out! Another thing struck me as being strange, and that was the cooking of a joint of beef just to "eat cold." If one carved it hot, it didn't go as far. Of course we did have hot roast beef once a week, with huge Yorkshire puddings served first with gravy. As the war progressed and meat was rationed, even the farm dinners consisted of "Woolton pie" — almost devoid of meat — and fish cakes made with a little tin of salmon.

There was, as it happened, a romantic reason why I knuckled down to humdrum housework. I became engaged to Jack, and knew that our future together would entail a life of cleaning, cooking, and not nearly as much outside work as I would like. I seemed to remember him saying: 'Oh, don't worry about that, we'll be able to have a maid," but, alas, she never materialised!

32

As well as the invalid sister to care for, there were two "lads" who lived in the house. They ate their meals and sat (if they ever had time!) in a side kitchen. Tea was poured into pint-sized enamel mugs, and both the meat and pudding courses were eaten off the same plate. For breakfast they had cold fat bacon eaten with dry bread and followed by a choice of pies. These appeared at each meal to "fill up on," and there was always at least part of a pie left on the table. Otherwise one would be worried in case they hadn't had enough! As well as the perennial cheesecakes, jam pies, and ground rice, there would be custards, and when in season fruit fillings were popular. One lad came from a "poor meat 'ouse" where the pies were "rhubub all t'summer and rhubub jam pie all t'winter!"

Bread and butter with jam as found on our table was never offered to the men. Pie was considered much better for lasting in the stomach. No-one feared heart disease, and the townspeople were referred to as "nobbut narrow-chinned bread-and-butter townees!"

I loved to hear of life in Mrs. Megginson's young days on a Wold farm. She recalled being one of the first people to give the men a mug of tea with meals, as before that it was considered cheaper to let them drink basins of separated milk!

With the advent of the Milk Marketing Board many farmers in the thirties started to sell milk, rather than separate it and sell butter, which must have made a lot of work for little profit. The butter was beautifully made up into pound or half pound blocks shaped by "Scotch hands" and imprinted with individual patterns by pressing the ridged side of the "hands" on the edges of the block — alternating with a plain stamp and then "bars" or stripes formed by using the "hands" upright. Sometimes a pictorial stamp was pressed in the centre, and being a keen hunting man, Jack's grandfather Sykes chose a fox motif. When that butter appeared in the market it was known as "Tally-Ho."

Now, the Megginsons had a small herd of cows to milk, including a few precious pedigree Friesians given to Jack by his godfather, "Uncle J.O." Every pint was needed to swell the monthly milk cheque. I never knew how so few pints were stretched or watered down to keep family and men in drinks and puddings! This milk was in any case considered too rich for cooking use, as in the days of separating the "old" milk, as it was called (although actually perfectly fresh!) it was either used up in the house or fed to the pigs. This "cheap" commodity was greatly missed.

I was soon taught to deal with rabbits, hares and poultry, which needed skinning, plucking and "dressing." Not being a squeamish type, I didn't mind the messy part, though I am still not keen, even now, about dealing with all the blood and the smelly guts of hares.

Wash-days meant boiling the whites, and "dollying" with a zinc tub, but my work was mostly as assistant cook, "washer-upper," and house cleaner. There was no electricity of course, and lamps or candles were our only illumination. I spent many winter evenings sewing patchwork cushions in the dim lamp-light, listening to the old radio with batteries that needed "charging" at a garage — "accumulators" by name.

The men who lived in took their personal washing home, or to someone in the village who was glad to earn the extra "bob" by obliging in such matters. Clothes were not subject to frequent washing anyway, and most weeks there would only be shirt, socks and vest. Shirts had long "laps," underpants were seldom worn, and "best" shirts always had spare collars, attached by studs, and so lasted clean for a longer time.

Some farm men were still paid by the year — from one Martinmas to the next — and only needed the ocasional "sub" during the year, though the old Hiring Fairs had practically died out by war-time. The only holiday, apart from Christmas Day, was the last week in November.

The men had a big bare bedroom up a back staircase off the kitchen and they shared a double bed as was the general custom. Some strange remarks would be made about such ideas today! I suppose originally the idea was to save laundering the rough, unbleached twill sheets. There were odd bits of mats on the bare floor, and each man had a chamber pot to use at night. During the day they were expected to make use of the fold yard or a handy hedge. The privies down the garden were only for family use!

CHAPTER SIX

The war situation became grave as the "phoney" stage ended and, after Dunkirk, troops arrived in our village. We really felt we were part of it all, instead of just hearing news on the wireless. The poor, tired lads occupied hastily erected tents, or took over any available space in granaries or other farm buildings.

We gave up two bedrooms at one stage, as the officers liked to have their wives near them — so we also cooked and cleaned for them, with some help from the batmen. Sentries appeared in the village street, fixed bayonets were the order of the day, and the cry "Who goes there?" became familiar. A curfew was enforced, and we found ourselves within the five-mile restricted limit along the coast, so no visitors were allowed through without permits.

With invasion imminent, we looked out each morning from bedroom windows across the flat fields towards the sea. The absence of cliffs made this stretch of coast very vulnerable in spite of concrete blocks, barbed wire entanglements, and mine fields which had appeared in this area as quickly as mushrooms. Concrete posts were erected in the fields about fifty yards apart, to prevent gliders landing, and this added to the difficulties of cultivation. At this time, too, the little ruined cottage on the sand dunes was blown up as it was considered to be too obvious a landmark for the enemy. We listened to wireless news, expecting to see German parachutists dropping from the clouds, and there were rumours that in the case of invasion women and children would be sent inland.

In the midst of this gloomy summer we made a quick decision to marry! At least we might get a short time together, and as a married couple might stand more chance of not being separated, whatever horrors lay in the future.

The wedding was hastily arranged. "Good," I thought, "no guests," as I'd always felt marriages were just for the two people concerned! However, we did have Joan as a faithful help and bridesmaid, and Jack's old friend Les as best man. My family from Hull were not to be left out, and applied for a permit to attend the ceremony in Barmston church.

All the same it was, as we wished, a quiet affair, and after cake and wine at Manor House, we were then driven to Bridlington station to catch a train for the Lake District, which I had loved when joining Pam and her family during the school holidays.

There we had five blissful days — no sign of war up there, sunshine, beautiful scenery, and time to walk in the mountains, explore by bus, and wander or rest by lakes or streams. All too soon it was time to make the return journey and settle down again in our daily routine.

One night when Jack and I were fastening up the poultry at dusk we were also engrossed in tracking down a large rat which had been killing chickens. So, Jack had taken his gun, and suddenly a large rodent crossed a space between huts. A quick shot and it lay dead. "Good," I remarked as Jack bent to pick up the body. Then, to our amazement, an officer came running up. "Who fired that shot?" he demanded. Jack admitted that he had, and held up the rat. "My goodness, never do that again. A single shot is a warning sign" — a sort of "action stations" we gathered. So chastened we crept back to the house!

The Home Guard (Dad's Army) was formed in the district, and Jack actually got to the stage of being issued with uniform and doing a night on duty. He spent a night in a dugout with regular soldiers. However, he was so concerned about the fate of his unmilked cows that he was permitted to return home to get on with the milking. After that he was only put on fire-duty, which was easier.

Free time was limited, though we were quite happy to go round the sheep on fine evenings with the pony and dog. Occasionally we could take the little old car, shared with the Hydes, to Bridlington for shopping, and sometimes we saw a film. We delighted in collecting "bottom drawer" articles and gradually acquired all our kitchen utensils from Woolworths, cutlery too, and all at 6d each — some are still in use to this day! — though the town was gloomy in the blackout.

In the meantime, the air raids started in full force. A few incendiaries landed in the paddock, where the pony was grazing, and some nights the sky in the direction of Hull, thirty miles away, was brilliant with the light from burning buildings. As planes droned overhead at night we listened with bumping hearts to their engines, while trying to decide whether they were "theirs" or "one of ours"!

When "Double Summertime" was brought in as an extra daylight saving measure, Farmer Megginson strongly objected. "Mucking about with nature," he called it, and muttered grumpily

The author "shepherding" in 1940.

about "only to make things easier for townees" — so our clocks remained one hour forward! It could be very muddling, especially when going to catch the bus to Brid or having "company" for a meal, but we managed without too much confusion.

One never-to-be-forgotten afternoon, the menfolk were working down the fields, stooking corn, when a fierce air-battle started overhead. Terrified, they dived for shelter in a large dyke, crouching in the mud and huddling under a small stone bridge under the cart track.

Mother-in-law and I were busy in the kitchen when we heard the terrible din overhead. We rushed into the safety of a dark, windowless back passage between the kitchen and the hall. With the doors shut, we huddled in the dark for about half-an-hour. The rattle of machine guns was so loud and my imagination ran riot. I was convinced that the invasion had begun, and that Jerries with guns were already in our front garden.

Then, quite suddenly, all was quiet! Still feeling shaky, with wobbly legs, we left the passage, and anxiously peeped through the windows! Not a soul in sight! The sun still shone from a blue sky.

We hadn't too long to wait till the men came rushing in — all chatter and excitement now the danger was over. They, of course, had seen most of the action (when not too scared to look upwards), and knew that at least one Nazi fighter plane had crashed to the ground in the Hydes' fields between us and the sea.

The author and her husband out riding at Manor House, Fraisthorpe, shortly after their wedding in 1940.

The Hydes and their men had been in those fields all the time, and had had an even more harrowing experience. When they went to investigate the wreckage — which spread over a wide area — there was little left. One man picked up the glove from a flying suit, only to drop it as he saw a hand still in it! Yet all over Britain such battles were bravely fought that summer, and the threat of invasion gradually receded.

Mother-in-law, on a rare shopping visit to Brid, was caught in Woolworths when a bomb fell on the Britannia Hotel opposite, and she had to shelter under a counter.

There was no hope yet of a house of our own, but Uncle J.O. was a wonderful help with influence in the right place, and before long we got the tenancy from the following April of a very run-down farm of one hundred and forty-seven acres — and it was less than two miles away.

Our thoughts were now firmly fixed on the excitement of moving to a farm and home of our own. Mother-in-law was a great help once she had accepted the fact that a "townee" was capable of looking after her only son. She taught me to be thrifty and to always put the comfort and welfare of the men first. No thoughts of "Women's Lib"! The men supplied our living, and when in the house everything must be done to save them exertion! Mother-in-law certainly had had more than her share of work and worry, and at about this time lost her dearly loved younger daughter. I like to think I distracted her a little in her grief, as I was always interested in tales of her early life, and also in her love of broad Yorkshire anecdotes.

She had lost her mother when only four years old, and so had been brought up by her father, four brothers and a housekeeper. How sad that her mother, Emma Rachel, had only known the joy of a baby daughter for so short a time. Beilby Sykes, her father, had been the son of a mill owner — a grinding mill — and we still have the old ledger, which is very interesting. However, Beilby wanted to farm, and so went to the Wolds as a pupil until taking on the tenancy of Wharram Grange where he also indulged in his great passion for hunting and the breeding and selling of hunters.

In photographs he resembles King Edward VII and must have been quite a character. He took pride in keeping the farmhouse and garden very tidy, and when one "posh" client arrived to buy a hunter he remarked: "This is a nice place, Sykes. I expect a gentleman lived here at one time." "Not till I came," was the apt reply!

After leaving the boarding school in Driffield — there were plenty of such private establishments for young ladies in those days — mother-in-law had to take over the duties of housekeeper and look after father and four brothers, though only one actually became a farmer. The eldest was "Uncle J.O." who helped us so much.

Mother-in-law had great strength of character, tackling any job in and around the house, and working "all hours that God sends" to help keep the wolf from the door in hard times. It was only in extreme old age that her mental and physical strength failed.

The first preparations I did for our own house consisted of filling numerous pillows and cushions. Mother-in-law provided a new hen hut, the floor of which was knee-deep in feathers, well dusted with Keatings ("kills bugs, moths and beetles") and I sat in there, filling the ticking cases machined for the purpose, and carefully rubbed inside with damp soap to add to the feather-proof quality. Needless to say all pillows and cushions have lasted till this day!

We had little money to spare on household furniture, but were fortunate to be given several useful items from my old home, as my mother had had to leave Hull during the worst of the bombing and most of the furniture went into store, until she later bought a house in Bridlington. She still travelled daily to the shop in Hull until she retired in her late seventies.

Jack went to several farm sales to look for implements, and other equipment we would need, and one afternoon he returned with a "suite" in the trailer. He was proud to have purchased it for £1. I looked, and was not quite so thrilled! A black horse-hair couch — mahogany framed — and two chairs to match, one without arms, was not quite my choice, but it tested my ingenuity!

I bought cheerful, thick curtain material, and in usual slap-dash manner cut out covers and tacked them over the offending and prickly horse-hair. It was my first attempt at this sort of job, and I felt quite proud of the result as I'd bought braid and gimp-pins to finish off neatly — and the result was quite pleasing, though odd prickles still came through.

The couch was a great asset in our kitchen for resting weary bones, or for Jack to sleep on in lambing time, and later for children to have their mid-day rest. Many years later that couch was replaced by a superior model in strong moquette and that cost all of £6. With lack of foresight it was thrown out in the fifties, just before old sofas began to be much sought after!

At another farm sale a set of dining chairs plus a matching upholstered "lady's chair" were put up for auction. No bids at all. "What," cried the auctioneer, "won't anyone give me a bob? I'll throw in this mirror — cheap enough for firewood!" "Yes," called Jack, and came home in triumph with the greatest bargain yet!

Those six dining chairs had pleasantly carved backs, and when the seats had tie-on cretonne covers they looked very presentable. The larger chair was "upholstered" for bedroom use, and the pine-framed mirror was painted in the fashion of the day and used on a matching chest of drawers. They all lasted many years, and all visitors were shown the "seven-for-a-shilling-with-mirror-thrown-in" bargain and were suitably impressed.

The blacksmith's shop was always an interesting place, and I loved to mooch round and have a chat. That blacksmith, like many others, was a real character, but had given up shoeing. I took the pony to Barmston forge where the shoeing smith was an even greater character and told me such fascinating tales of his early days in a "Big House" that the pony seemed to be shod in no time! However, in the Fraisthorpe shop, I spied a Windsor chair. It was firm, and strong, but covered in red varnish. Yes, he would sell it to me — also a little side table with a drawer, and a bedroom chair. How much? Ten bob the lot!

I returned home, very thrilled. It was the first of many such jobs in "stripping" and very rewarding when the mellow tone of good old elm was revealed, and my Windsor chair to this day is a cherished possession. The little table and chair I regret to say I painted in the fashion of the moment.

My friend Joan persuaded her father to sell her a mahogany rocking chair, again paying ten shillings, and this she gave to us as I fancied one in our kitchen. This, also when the red varnish was removed, proved a beautiful chair, and is also in our home, and promoted to sitting room use!

We went to Hull one day, and looked at carpets in Bladons furniture department. The price frightened us, as we needed several, but a kindly salesman came to our assistance with a quantity of good quality but second-hand carpets and rugs removed from a bombed house. The price was right, and all fitted perfectly into plans for our new home. A large slightly worn Indian, another large and good Belgian weave, two large oriental rugs, and two lengths of good Axminster known as "corridor rugs." Thirty pounds the lot, and they gave very good service.

CHAPTER SEVEN

I must admit that when I first saw Kingsfield my heart sank. From the outside it was quite pleasant — long, rather than square, the usual type of local farmhouse architecture, perhaps older than some, and the lower, back kitchen end was joined on to the buildings. There was a brick porch over the front door, a small garden with tall white poplar trees and at the back a sloping roof covered two small bedrooms with dairies underneath.

We were only permitted one look round inside, prior to our move, a concession to enable us to meaure windows for curtains and black-out blinds. The previous tenants lived in gipsy style. Two brothers and a sister, all elderly, and satisfied with primitive conditions.

They had refused to be connected to mains water, though they had agreed to a Yorkist range being put in the front kitchen. We entered via a dirty and dingy back entrance with a window-less porch, and the light didn't improve much in the back kitchen, where a small window looked on to a little concrete area beside the big fold-yard. My first thought was: "I'll be as blind as a pit pony if I have to live here," but, knowing we were fortunate to get a farm near enough Manor House for us to share implements, I decided I must make the best of this gloomy place and endeavour to turn it into a comfortable home.

The tour of the house to measure windows did little to enhance the first impression. The front kitchen was lighter, or would be when gloomy blue distempered walls were painted. The middle room through which one walked to the staircase, and the far sitting room plus three dairies completed the ground floor. Fireplaces in the rooms had obviously not been used for years, and were in a bad state, with broken grates.

There were three good-sized bedrooms upstairs, with two small ones which had sloping ceilings and very damp walls. From the dark back kitchen the "men's staircase" led to a bedroom with a minute window at floor level as the ceiling sloped at that end to within two feet of the floorboards.

A sour smell pervaded the house, and a large wooden butter churn in the front kitchen may have been responsible for this, plus the fact that the windows had remained closed for many years.

The author's interpretation of "Kingsfield."

Lady Day, April 6th, was the day for moving to new farms. The previous tenants moved out before mid-day, so it was early afternoon when we drove there, along the main road and down the little winding lane I was soon to know so well, followed by two trailer-loads of household furniture and previous chattels.

The mess left in the house was incredible, and we — yes, mother-in-law was with me — could only stare in horror, but dear Uncle J.O. had arrived a short time before and was tackling the brick floor of the front kitchen with a stable broom (!) plus buckets of water.

One of the farm lads who came down with a trailer looked around in amazement: "By, it may be Kingsfield, but it beant King's 'ouse." We ran from room to room exclaiming at the neglect, and Uncle J.O., in his official role of under-agent, left his floor cleaning to make notes to report to his estate boss.

Mother-in-law (coarse apron needed here!) was soon tackling the scrubbing after making sure the copper didn't leak before lighting up a fire underneath. Quite surprisingly it held water, which soon heated up.

There was a large old black range in the back kitchen with a side boiler and a "reckon" on which we could hang a kettle, though I felt a witches' cauldron would have been more appropriate. This range also had an ashpit under a grating, but Uncle J.O. soon had that filled in. We also had a wall oven similar to the one at Manor Farm, but it never worked well. It must have been installed by an inefficient bricklayer — so we didn't use it.

The only sink, in front of the little window in this back kitchen — quite a large place with a concrete floor — was quite unusable! Made of stone, and very shallow, it was "bunged up," and when we prodded around the outlet pipe, water just gushed through to the floor below. The colour of the water which came from the pump over the sink was so brown that we decided not to risk drinking it, so someone rushed back to the village for a milk churn of fresh water. For several weeks our supply was brought in that fashion.

The investigation of the "privy" on the house-end was another shock. The door was off its hinges, and an elderberry sapling grew drunkenly across the threshold. No signs of this dirty place having been in recent use — they must have preferred the fold yard — so this was priority No. 1.

Another trip to the village, and this emergency was solved when Henry offered a camping toilet left by caravan owners when removing their caravan at the outbreak of war. The tin "sentry box" arrived on a rulley complete with Elsan container. Set up at the back of the house in a rather public place, it at least solved our problem , and remained there for a long time.

The next job was to make the kitchen clean enough to eat in. Mother-in-law scraped off muck before she could start scrubbing the Yorkist range, doors and cupboard shelves. I did likewise in the dairy, where all our food would be stored. There was also a "milk" dairy, and one opening off the middle room which had better walls and shelves, and rather grandly became the "china pantry" where best pots and wedding present china were set out.

I had painted (did I ever put my brush down?) a wooden kitchen dresser, and, with the little side table and large central table (which cost a pound), plus our couch and chairs, we were "set up." A rag rug covered part of the floor, which proved to be good red brick when clean.

A kitchen in a farmhouse today would cost at least a thousand pounds! What a constant trail we had to and fro to the sink in the other kitchen, when we got a usable one, but we hadn't long to wait for that, or for mains water.

We had the most respectable bedroom sufficiently clean to erect our bed. There was no thought of not sleeping there that night. We had our stock to see to! We had eight Friesian cows, twenty-three ewes, three pigs, and a dozen hens — the last a present from Jack's married sister. We also had a lovely chestnut carthorse called Sharper, and so couldn't leave them, once installed in new quarters or pastures. Jack was also keen to be "boss" on his own farm too.

Tired to the point of exhaustion, we were eventually alone in our new home, and plodded up the bare stairs in the dark. We couldn't use a candle as the paper blinds necessary for the blackout hadn't been fixed, and of course the new curtains wouldn't be hung till the rooms were decorated. Luckily our sense of humour hadn't left us, and we giggled as we undressed, especially when Jack kept muttering that he couldn't find the bed post on which he always hung his trousers — no wonder, we had changed beds!

The next morning we discovered cockroaches, or "black clocks" in local language! Both kitchens were swarming with these horrid insects. There was an S.O.S. for Keatings, which helped, as we swept up shovelfuls each morning after that. A few always lurked in corners, and it took a long time for me to break the habit of turning all cups, glasses and mugs upside down on the cupboard shelf. We also caught a few mice, and suffered from the odd flea bite in the early days!

We had to get the men's bedroom, and back kitchen, habitable within a few days before our new man, Charlie, came to start work. Once more Joan came to help, as she had done to improve our Manor House bedroom before we married, and we hurriedly painted all the doors, including the cupboard under the back stairs, and slapped distemper on the rough walls. The table, chairs and dresser in here had all been in kitchen quarters in Hull. We used a dark "engine" green for woodwork, and buff for the walls.

On the Monday, the ever-faithful Lill came for the day by bus from Hornsea where she and mother had a temporary home. She thought it all a bit rough, but was ready to tackle any job, which was wonderful.

We had to go back to Manor House for baths, and I think they "pumped up" for us, but gradually things improved. I was particularly grubby the day the Agent — considered an important person — called on us. I was scrubbing the floor at the time, and almost the first thing he said was: "I think you must have a bathroom!" But in spite of my hints in that direction, he wouldn't agree to a w.c.! The septic tank would cost over one hundred pounds. We never thought of being able to afford such a large amount, and neither did the Agent, so that was a luxury we had to forgo.

We were soon connected to mains water, and a back boiler was put behind the Yorkist range. A lovely shiny white sink with taps was installed in the back kitchen. The estate workmen were good, if slow, and Uncle J.O. was there to supervise, and also soon made a start at digging the derelict vegetable garden behind some buildings, and in no time, it seemed, planted fruit bushes, raspberry canes and vegetables.

A lad cycled daily from the village, and Jack worked outside as long as daylight lasted. We had a local man to put wallpaper on the bedroom walls while I kept on painting all the woodwork in various colours. I was determined not to have it all "drab" — a favourite shade for farmhouse interiors at that time. Until the bathroom was finished, the other little "lean-to" room became a "wash-place" with an old wash-stand, bowl and jug set.

We soon had friends and family coming for a meal or to stay a few days. Joan, Les, and one or two school friends now living some distance away, braved the lack of comfort and amenities to find out what sort of a place we were living in. Looking back, they must have had quite a shock! Even many years later when we felt quite civilised, a friend of the willow tree era came to tea. Looking round that awful kitchen she remarked: "Oh dear, what a change from Newland Park!" She too had married a farmer "down south," so yet another family with common interests became good friends.

In that first summer at Kingsfield we had only the kitchen in which to sit, not that there was much time for that, as the sitting room fireplace was not installed until autumn.

We had the bathroom in use by July, and what a pride and joy that was — white painted walls (at home bathrooms and toilets had always been white) with patterned linoleum on the floor, and check gingham curtains.

We even installed an "Eltex" loo in one corner — to the consternation of the old bricklayer who had to fix a ventilation pipe. He didn't approve of "them things" indoors, and solemnly taking

47

up position on the seat — I wanted it across a corner — he looked up and in a deadpan voice enquired: "Noo, are you going to 'ave plenty of elbow-room?" a remark that has remained as a family joke.

I must admit that it was much better than the sentry-box, but it often caused a crisis when it needed emptying when there were visitors around. Not the easiest thing to carry downstairs and through three doors before reaching the yard, and more than once there were occasional splashes to remove from the stair carpet!

We were really quite proud of our sitting-room when it was ready for use. Mother had provided a good quality, silvery wallpaper, the tiled fireplace provided by the estate was plain and innocuous, and I painted the doors in mahogany gloss! We still felt that light paint showed the dirt quickly.

We had been given the old chesterfield and winged chairs from the Hull dining room — peacock blue plush with a colony of moths, acquired in storage, which caused a long war against the grubs! There were odd springs which dug into one's anatomy, but it was a pleasing shape and looked very smart in new loose covers. The material, a strong linen in Jacobean pattern, cost five shillings a yard, and was made by an odd little woman who lived in a tall house overlooking Brid harbour — rather like perpetually living on a ship. We felt we'd been quite extravagant in having such luxurious material.

She also made the covers for our "seven-for-a-shilling" dining chairs which stood round a good mahogany dining table with leaves. We found this for five pounds in Kilham. We had odd bits and pieces which we had received as wedding presents, and a bookcase for my precious theatrical and horsey books. Later we acquired a corner cupboard as a "bad debt." The pictures were mostly Peter Scott prints, which were fashionable at that time. Curtains were adapted from the new ones we'd hung in our Manor House bedroom. With our "bargain" carpet and "stained surrounds" we felt it was all quite luxurious!

In the midst of all this settling in period, we were happy to work long hours and to gradually improve things indoors and out. Jack was milking three times a day to get the highest yields, and we still used a pair of carthorses, though we had a new tractor, a generous gift from Uncle J.O. It was a Massey 101, and a proud possession.

Our chestnut carthorse, Sharper, had cost sixty-five guineas, and was a first-class horse. Charlie was so thrilled to use him. "As sensible as a christian," was his comment. Land work was laborious, with the hand hoeing of turnips, swedes and kale. Chopping thistles out of corn was known as "luking," and I've since heard that this strange expression comes from the Danish word for a hoe.

Haymaking was a chancey job in poor weather, and haycocks were made after raking the hay into rows for swaths which were turned by hand. Soon we were able to borrow the new "sweep," which was a great invention. We grew wheat, oats and barley, and were glad when our first harvest was safely stacked, and I was called on to help as a "picker" again.

One field was rough pasture with lots of gorse bushes. I loved it, a "real picnic place," but before long this was ploughed and drained and produced good crops. The fields were mostly surrounded by high, untidy hedges, wonderful for brambles, but gradually these were chopped down and neatly laid, giving more land to cultivate. The dykes needed cleaning, and thigh-high rubber boots were worn for this job, when the men almost disappeared from sight.

We had been given an old Humber car by a generous relative, and could go shopping in Brid when petrol permitted, as it was strictly rationed. The blackout made the town strange and eerie at night, and of course all signposts had been removed, so one did not venture far into strange countryside.

I didn't drive, but was good on a bike! The three miles to Brid seemed quite a long way if there was a head wind, and I could also use the buses which passed the lane end. My mother and Lill now lived in Brid, and Lill valiantly came out to help me on washing days, and also with the "big bake" on Fridays. Looking back, I don't know how I would have coped without her "voluntary" help, and I was thankful to be able to care for her in her old age.

Washing was really a heavy job to tackle single-handed. First the copper had to be filled and the fire lit under it. It was boiling by the time Lill arrived at 9.30. Dirty clothes were scrubbed in the wooden wash-tub, which was brought out to stand in the shallow sink. Other items were put in the zinc dolly-tub, and the suds were agitated by twisting and twirling the dolly-stick which had three wooden legs sticking out from the round base at the end of the shaft. Hard exercise, and the job was repeated with clean water when rinsing.

The "whites" were boiled in the copper, and the towels. Some things needed starching, so a bowl of this glutenous substance was mixed. A blue bag was added to the final rinsing water for those precious whites. Yes, we were very particular, and took pride in this lengthy process. I'd been given an old Acme rubber roller wringer, so I never had to struggle with a wooden mangle.

How glad we were when the weather was kind and the clothes could be hung out to dry. Otherwise they were slung up over the fireside on a big wooden airer on a pulley, or draped over a heavy clothes-horse, or "winter-hedge" as some people would say. Uncle J.O. had made both airer and clothes-horse and made sure they were strong enough to "take a few blankets," so they were heavy to handle! It was quite an achievement to get dried and ironed before bedtime, and I was often "at it" till late in the evening.

The iron was a luxury-type "flat" variety, known as a box-iron. Lill found it on a market stall, and it proved a good buy. I am only sorry that I once lent it to an exhibition of "by-gones" and was careless about getting it back. It had two heavy iron "innards," as I called them, which were dropped into the hot coals of the range. When red, they were fished out with the hooked end of a special rod and deftly dropped into the hollow iron. The lid was then clamped down, and away we went. Clonk-clonk as the iron moved over the linen or clothes, but I felt it was worth the trouble to avoid the black marks which sometimes appeared when using the ordinary flat iron. I thought it all rather primitive after the electric irons at home, though the early models had to be switched on and off to control the heat.

The sheets had always to be correctly folded, and there was a lot of pulling and stretching between two people to get the ends straight and in line ready for ironing. They were mostly plain sheets, with perhaps a drawn-thread insertion for "best" or even a hand-embroidered monogram, but even the men's "twill" had to be "straight" to fold away in the linen chest.

CHAPTER EIGHT

By the middle of that first summer at Kingsfield I discovered I was pregnant, but in the manner of that time I tried to ignore the fact. No-one talked of such things to a young girl. My sisters, who were so much older, had had babies, but I had taken little notice (one was in Canada at the time) and had always been more drawn to dogs or horses! Jack, who loved small children, said: "Don't worry, I'll help with it, and I can talk to babies."

Luckily I was well, and didn't think of going to our doctor — who incidentally was more of a friend, and stabled his hunter at Manor House — until I developed a kidney infection. I summoned up the courage to mention the pregnancy, and re-reading old diary entries for that day read: "Dr. very nice about other thing." I couldn't even write it!

This may seem strange to younger readers, but there were no magazine articles on such delicate subjects, and novels I'd read glossed over births until the heroine was brought to bed. None of my close friends were even married, so there was no help there. I just carried on the daily round as usual, feeling very self-conscious about my ever-increasing girth. I eventually booked into the maternity home and hoped for the best!

I didn't mention my condition, other than to the family and close friends, and eventually the butcher who brought our meat twice weekly could wait no longer: "I don't wish to be personal my dear, but shouldn't you be giving me your extra coupons?"

Lill told me I must buy material for baby nighties — the sort that lasted from birth till two years. These were machined for me, and mother got out her knitting needles. I bought a dreadfully unbecoming "maternity" dress from a catalogue which cost precious clothing coupons. Otherwise I wore smocks — passed on by my sister — over skirts with elastic to bridge the gap when they no longer fastened in the normal manner.

We didn't light fires in the sitting room except at weekends, so we sat in the kitchen in the early part of that winter during the dark evenings. Sometimes Charlie sat in with us, unless cycling to Brid, and we listened to the wireless. The programmes were really funny, or perhaps they meant a lot to us, deprived of other entertainment. The war news was a constant anxiety, and we seldom missed a

51

bulletin. Sometimes bombs were dropped near enough to cause alarm, but we were fortunate to be so far from Hull, which suffered very badly throughout the war.

Uncle J.O. walked into the house with a little Christmas tree in mid-December: "I thought you'd want a tree, Irene." Well, I thought, a nice idea, but what do I do with it! However, I found a few beads, and bits of jewellery and ribbons, and it looked quite pretty. I remember that Christmas mostly for having the luxury of the sitting room fire for two days and going up to Manor House for our Christmas dinner. The middle room, which was to be our everyday sitting room and "nursery," was waiting for the estate men to put in the fireplace, and in January they made a start.

At the same time Jack had to take a Friesian cow to the special sale at York, and this meant being away for a night. He was rather concerned about leaving me, with just Charlie in the house. If I didn't feel well I had to send a message up to Manor House before mother-in-law and Uncle J.O. left for York in the morning as they were going by car. I didn't worry, saying: "Oh, first babies are always late." Where had I got that idea? Anyway, I wasn't due for another week.

Well, I had a very disturbed night, but felt it was my "kidney ache" again, so I got up and saw to Charlie's breakfast as usual. I felt more ill, but on looking at the clock realised mother-in-law would have left by that time.

The two bricklayers were busy with the new fireplace, so I made them "looance." I then decided we needed bread, so I mixed the dough and left it to rise. I gave Charlie some dinner, but didn't feel hungry myself. Eventually, passing the workmen with a ghastly smile I went upstairs to lie on my bed, still convinced I had kidney trouble. After all, I wasn't doing what cows did, and I'd formed my idea of childbirth from watching them!

An hour or so later, feeling sick and shivery, I decided I must see a doctor, so I struggled out to the cowhouse where George, our lad who helped to milk, looked at me with concern. I asked him to cycle to the village, and if our doctor wasn't riding (he often did so on Tuesdays) he had to ask the Hydes to phone. George was off up that lane like a shot!

I paced around till he returned with the message that the Hydes' car would be here soon and I had to go to the maternity home. John, a bachelor, looked rather worried as I staggered to the car, clutching my case. I'd been washing the hearth and felt grubby, and I had also left the bread in the oven, but by then I was past caring!

I was received at the hospital by a sister of the "battle-axe" breed, who looked at me and said: "I'm going for my tea, wait here." I really was very uncomfortable, and could hardly sit on the chair. Other people were in this waiting-room, and one remarked: "Serve that old girl right if it's born on the floor!"

I was collected after a short time and propelled along the corridor where, to my relief, I met "Dear Doctor" hurrying in. "Oh, I'm so glad to see you. I hope this isn't a false alarm!" I still didn't think things were progressing towards the actual birth!

I wasn't left in doubt for long. They hardly had time to get me to the labour ward, and half-an-hour later they told me I had a son! It had all been quite horrifying, in spite of Dear Doctor being so kind, but as soon as it was over I felt fine, and very hungry.

It was lovely to be in a comfortable bed. The nurse who brought water for washing was surprised by the state of my work-stained hands! I'd never really thought of giving them a scrub after doing the hearth.

Meanwhile the cow, Margaret, had been sold and Jack returned home with mother to hear the news of my departure! Much use was made of the Hydes' phone, and soon my worried-looking husband was at my bedside listening to my tale of woe. He was thrilled, of course, to have a son, and as Margaret had made £112 and I had been promised all over a hundred, I felt rich indeed!

I heard of Charlie's concern for me and how he'd gone into the kitchen, smelt the bread, and had taken it out of the oven. He proudly said he'd "knapped loaves on t'bottom" as he turned them out of the tins, "Cos I'd seen Missus do it!" If a hollow sound was heard one knew they were ready.

Very different from today's mums, I didn't see baby Anthony till the next morning and could only think of Henry VIII as an old man. I'd seen Charles Laughton in the film five times, and this little baby had such a wise old expression on his crinkly face. Jack didn't see him for four nights. He didn't want to waste our precious visiting hour in queueing up to peep in at the nursery door! "I shall see him all the time when we get him home." Dear me, what would the modern school of thought make of that, when fathers are expected to hold one's hand throughout the whole business and babies are kept beside the mums all the time.

I would still want to be free of my nearest and dearest when in labour, and throughout the messy business of giving birth!

I enjoyed the peace of a single room, reading, writing long letters, having visitors, embroidering little flowers on baby nighties and pillow slips! Breast feeding was no problem, and I usually read during this restful occupation. We were not permitted to put a foot out of bed for ten days, and then I had the joy of getting into normal clothes, walking round the hospital garden, and learning to bath and change my baby.

I felt weak and wan on my return home. Lots of work seemed to be waiting, groceries had to be put away, tea got ready, and what about the baby? Jack, as predicted, was perfectly at home with him, nursing and talking to him like an old hand at the game.

Dear Doctor had given orders to feed by the clock — four-hourly — not to pick up in between and to "hold out" on a basin after each feed! I stuck to these instructions, and gradually got into the new routine. We had a few broken nights, but if it was not feeding time Jack would say: "Don't worry, he has all day to sleep in, and you haven't!"

Of course it was cold in January in the farmhouse near the East Coast, where the only heating was the kitchen range and an oil stove. The latter was portable and very useful. Mother-in-law had papered the "nursery" so I had a fire in the new grate where I could sit in private at feeding times. No-one worried about Tony sleeping in an unheated bedroom. The cradle was warmed first with a hot water bottle, then a well-wrapped babe was tucked in. The window was open a crack too, as fresh air was considered important. I got all my baby-care knowledge from the "Mother-craft Manual" I'd been given, and I followed advice blindly, though later I referred to it as "the daft book Mummie gave me!"

The pram was pushed into the garden or front porch after the 10 a.m. feed, and the baby stayed there except for feed times until dark. If a feed was nearly due and I could hear yells, I brought him in and carried on with jobs, such as setting the table, with him tucked happily under my arm. I became quite good at working in this manner!

Only fog was said to be harmful, otherwise the pram was out of doors. The porch was useful in wet weather, and Jack made a wire-netting cover to keep cats from jumping on the pram.

We were both highly delighted with our wee son, who soon

Tony's christening in 1943.

started to smile back at us, and to play with wooden beads tied to the pram hood. Life became even more of a rush with all the nappies and wet nighties. There were no plastic pants, and my book said rubber ones were unhealthy.

The cooking, cleaning and baking had to go on as usual, and the meals, especially Charlie's, had to be put on the table "on the dot"! Lill's visits on Mondays and Fridays were greatly appreciated. She loved the baby, and as he grew older she brought gifts to amuse him.

When Tony was a few weeks old I pushed the pram up to Manor House to help with a threshing day. Threshing days were dreaded on farms, both indoors and out. In my day it was always pulled by a tractor — a Field Marshall — but not long before a traction engine had been necessary, and the men liked it in place the night before to enable them to have plenty of time to get "steam up" before starting at seven o'clock. So, sticking to tradition, they arrived at night in time for tea and expected their breakfast the next morning too! The starting time had been put forward to 7.30 a.m.

Extra men were borrowed from neighbouring farms, so the work force was considerably increased and "looance" often needed for twelve men. There were corn carriers, "caff" carriers, two on the straw stack, two on the corn stack, and two on the machine, plus an engine man.

It was all dust and sweat! The poor "caff" staggered from caff heap to barn almost obscured from sight by the big sheets of sacking which they struggled to keep on their backs while holding the four corners. Only strong chaps could carry corn in heavy sacks, the weight varying from twelve stone of oats, sixteen of barley, and eighteen of wheat. It took toll of those men, even when they were physically strong, and many, including Jack, had overdeveloped shoulders as a result of humping those weighty bags up the granary steps.

At midday all trouped into the farm kitchens to be fed with huge meat and tatie pies, followed by a giant-sized rice pudding. At least this was the most popular and quickly served dinner. Great mugs of tea helped to wash it all down, and there were, of course, the plate pies to make sure everyone had had their fill.

Before the washing-up was done and the two tables (in front and back kitchens) cleared, it was time to think about the afternoon "looance." The basket of food, enamel mugs, plus the big can of tea had to be ready promptly at three o'clock.

Unless there was a second day's threshing, one thankfully watched the machine chug off to another farm where tea would be waiting for the two men — if not, the same routine went on for another day, and one had to have bacon cakes ready for the next morning's "looance" at 9.30 a.m. No wonder, when I first heard of combine-harvesters, all I could think of was "no more threshing days!"

As the work force of men was depleted by the calling-up process, Land Army girls were detailed to follow the machines. Poor lasses! What a job! They, however, brought a packed lunch, and I can see them now, sitting in a row on our old couch. I couldn't leave them out-of-doors, and I also provided a drink. They looked so dusty, covered with chaff, and bits of straw, and I wondered what their landladies thought of lodgers who left a trail of "bits" all over their houses!

After Tony grew into a lively toddler, absolutely obsessed by anything on wheels and preferably with an engine, he liked to stand on the kitchen window sill behind the old couch where he could see down the lane. He jogged up and down with excitement, shouting: "Fashing sheen coming, fashing sheen coming!" At least we had someone who welcomed the wretched thing!

The harvest of 1943 was unforgettable, as we were offered help from the Army. Both farms, Manor House and Kingsfield, had corn ready for "leading," and members of the Tank Corps, still stationed in the village, were not fully occupied. What a difference it made to have not only the soldiers but some trucks! Some days there would be eight extra men, and sometimes as many as twenty. We might get four trucks, or no trucks, and sometimes neither. I suppose it was a great boon when all turned up, and never had the stacks grown so quickly as when loads of sheaves were chucked willy nilly into the deep-bottomed lorries. No carefully balanced loading needed on this occasion.

The main problem, of course, was the baking. We were nearly driven mad with the problem of supplying enough food, but mother-in-law, Lill, and myself all worked together over this sudden increase in numbers for "looances."

There were, mercifully for us, the odd wet days when we could draw breath. I especially remember how happy the soldiers were to be helping, and some would peep at Tony as he kicked and gurgled in his pram, under the poplar tree on our little front lawn. Perhaps he reminded them of their own babies, so very seldom seen.

One day, as I rushed around from one job to another, a cheery fellow with a Scottish accent came into the kitchen with his shirt over his arm. Could I possibly put in a few wee stitches where he'd nearly ripped out the sleeve? I ran for my sewing box, feeling life was becoming more and more like one long obstacle race!

We had an unexpected bonus for our rations too, as a couple of cooks smuggled us a box of dried fruit. Corn in Egypt indeed! We could almost count the number of currants we'd been putting into teacakes or curd tarts.

Joan was a frequent weekend visitor, and always ready to lend a hand either indoors or out, though I think she was somewhat appalled by my ever-increasing domesticity which was rather overwhelming at times. She once remarked that whenever she was with us it was always time to do some job or other.

CHAPTER NINE

Of course we made the house as safe as we could for a young child. We used a play-pen to keep small knees off cold floors, and later fixed a board in slots across the nursery doorway to keep the toddler safely in there, yet able to look through to the kitchen to talk or see what was going on. The cold brick floor wasn't a suitable surface for a little one to play around, and they didn't wear trousers in those days! The so-called "buster-suits" were not at all practical, even if sweet to look at!

The stairs had a gate fixed at the top, and the bottom could be shut off as there wasn't a hall. When busy upstairs I found that gate invaluable. By this time I had a good help on two afternoons a week for the cleaning of bedrooms and dairies. It all seems, looking back, as if we were far too particular about sweeping, dusting and scrubbing. However, when everything was so primitive, with no short-cut methods, it's surprising how long each job could take. What a lot of walking too, with no sink in the kitchen where most of the work was done, and there was a constant need to fetch or take things to and from the dairies.

About this time we had a great improvement in our cooking arrangements. A two-burner Calor gas stove with a grill was bought and installed on a little table near the kitchen range with the cylinder sitting underneath. What luxury! It was such a joy to poach eggs and stir custard without the danger of smuts dropping in. The pans got so black on the fire too, and inclined to burn on one side. Now I could grill sausages or chops when we could get them, and that single little cooking stove was the most labour-saving gadget I'd ever had. We now had two lads living in, so it was a great asset.

Rationing caused many a headache, though we were never short of food. We had eggs and poultry, and the odd rabbit. Meat was seldom off the menu as we had a crafty butcher. Although still short of money for luxuries, food didn't seem dear, and the bills were always paid without worry.

Making enough pastry was the most difficult job, with all fats in short supply. The pies, I'm afraid, were often tough, even by "farm lad" standards. Sometimes it was hard to keep a selection of fillings, as plenty of changes were expected. We could get a basin of fresh curd in the village for tuppence, and this, mixed with sugar, eggs and currants, was a good standby, but needed to be eaten fresh in those pre-fridge and freezer days.

Mother-in-law talked of the days when farm lads would leave a penny on the plate when a pie was mouldy — inferring that it needed a shave!

The grocer who came each fortnight for orders was a serious-faced, elderly man with a monotonous voice. He read from his list with suggestions, always ending with "Mrs. 'erh" after each recital of commodities. Even now I smile at the thought of that dear man! He was so tactful when he called at a time when I was busy breast-feeding. If in the kitchen I shot through to the nursery with the babe still clinging on, and, out of breath, I would call: "I'm busy with baby," and he'd reply: "Quite alright, don't worry! Now what about flour Mrs. 'erh?"

We could fill in forms to apply for extra rations for jobs when "looance" was needed — hay-time, harvest, muck-leading, sheep-shearing and threshing days. "Oh yes," he'd say, "and don't forget to put your name as you need extra for getting it all ready, Mrs. 'erh." Yet what a luxury it was to have the order carried through to the kitchen table and unpacked. No pushing a trolley round a supermarket and carrying the stuff in from the car.

We always ordered salt in a block, apart from a little Saxa for the table. A block had to be chiselled with a large knife and the pieces crushed with a rolling-pin before storing it in stone jars. We needed a lot, of course, when it was time to kill a pig.

During the war one could get permits for this purpose, and two were allowed per year, though naturally surreptitious slaughtering did take for black market supplies, and we heard tales of narrow escapes and some prosecutions. We preferred to play safe, and kept within the law.

There was usually a man locally who specialised in the art of pig-killing, and he was booked to come on a specified day. The poor pig was soon slaughtered and hung up on the "caumbrill," the skin scraped, and the "fry" brought indoors. There was a strange custom about giving a plate of "fry" (liver, heart and kidneys) to a neighbour — the plate must be returned unwashed or bad luck would follow! It seemed rather odd to me. People were very glad of this tasty addition to the meat ration.

The following day, the chap returned to cut up the carcass. The sides of bacon and the hams were salted down, usually laid on the brick floor under the dairy shelves and left for three weeks. More salt and saltpetre and brown sugar might be added during this period. The delicious back-bone joints known as "chine" and the spare ribs were soon roasted. They tasted extra sweet and good, and the bones were well-sucked so that not a scrap was wasted.

We especially loved pork pies, so all the minced meat went into these rather than putting some into sausages. The head, trotters and tail were made into brawn.

With no fridges, this all had to be "sided" quickly, so it was a busy week indeed. The "leaf" fat (from around the kidneys) was considered the best for pastry making, so it was all chopped into little squares and rendered in the oven. What lovely lard it made, all poured off into stone jars, and the residue of crispy little fragments were called "scraps," which some folk thought a treat. The rest of the fat was treated in the same way — good lard, but not the best quality.

The brawn-making entailed long, slow cooking in large sauce-pans, or even in the copper, and when cool it was strained, and the fiddly business began of separating meat from bone and unappetising bits of skin, gristle or hairs! We chopped the ears too, as we were loathe to waste anything. It all set in a professional-looking mould when turned out. If I make it today when a pig comes for the freezer, I only use the best bits of meat. What would mother-in-law say today? The brawn was eaten with a sprinkling of sugar, and vinegar was poured over every slice.

Pie-making was a big baking day, and much fuss and worry went into getting them just right and the oven the correct temperature. The crust was mixed with boiling milk, and pig's foot jelly was added to the coarsely minced pork. Seasoned with salt and pepper, it was packed into the pastry-lined tins (no, I never tried "raised" pies) and the tops were decorated with pastry leaves or twisted strips. Baked fast at first and then slowly — what a delicious smell, and how lovely they looked when brushed with beaten egg.

It is very hard to believe, but the most we ever made was seventeen pies of various sizes, and they kept fresh for three weeks before the last morsel was eaten. We gave away a few, of course, but in a cold dairy (they always faced north) I suppose the pastry sealed the meat from contact with impurities, as we never made a hole in the top to add more jelly. Anyway, they were all eaten, and no-one suffered from tummy-ache!

The hams and sides of bacon were duly hung on the hooks in the kitchen ceiling, much admired by callers. "The prettiest picture you'll ever see," was a favourite comment. I was glad to have the extra meat, but didn't really care for the fatty ham or bacon. Sometimes I thought it "reasty" — but then I still had some "townee" fads.

Bacon cakes the size of the oven shelf were a constant favourite for morning "looance." Very simple to make, just two large circles of pastry with chopped bacon scattered over one piece, pepper added, and the second circle put on top. The edges were damped with milk and the top brushed in the same way and baked till golden brown with the bacon bits well frizzled inside. I still make a small version with shop bacon, and beaten egg used rather than milk.

We often had a few visitors to see us and to join us for meals, and in 1943 mother-in-law had new paying guests. An air-force sergeant, Jim, and his wife Mary had recently married, and naturally didn't like the idea of Mary returning to their native Liverpool. Jim was stationed at Lissett aerodrome only a few miles from Manor House, so there they settled, in the rooms vacated by the army officers, and became our life-long friends!

Each Saturday evening they walked to visit us, had a simple fireside supper and lots of lively conversation, then retraced their steps down the lane. This routine lasted till Mary went back to Liverpool for the birth of their first baby, and later still the new mother returned with the little girl, when mother-in-law would baby-sit on Saturday nights so that our supper parties could continue.

Lambing time meant longer working hours than ever for Jack, who was shepherd as well as cowman, plus general worker. When "sitting up" with the ewes — our flock had increased from the original twenty to seventy — he snatched what sleep he could on that invaluable couch. The fold yard was near the house, far too near for my liking, but easy for looking after sheep, in the section specially partitioned off, with small pens for those with new lambs.

It was rewarding work and, being a good shepherd, Jack took pride in having healthy ewes and a good crop of lambs. Every small, wrinkly, wobbly-legged little creature was important and must be saved if possible. Sometimes a very weak one would be cosseted in a box in front of the fire — and what a feeling of triumph if it gained strength and I returned to the kitchen to find it bleating and making a little pool on the rug as it endeavoured to stagger across the floor.

Sometimes a lot of patience was needed when a ewe, for some reason only known to herself, turned against one of her pair. All tricks were tried to encourage her to welcome it again. Perhaps putting both lambs in a barrel for an hour or two and then bringing them both together to suckle while the ewe was tied up. If one of the lambs died and another was offered for the ewe to foster, it would be dressed in the skin taken from the dead one (not a pleasant job) and this deception usually worked. After a few days the rather disgusting skin could be removed when hopefully the foster child was accepted.

As the lambs grew stronger and were able to live in the paddock, we liked to watch them skipping around playing happy games in the spring sunshine. Of course we also got spells of un-spring like weather when they shivered miserably around their mothers, and we worried that they might have to be brought under cover again.

Uncle J.O., on his frequent visits, was very good with children, and all the little ones took to him straight away. "Come on," he'd say to Tony, "let's go and see those little lambs." Another time it would be the "chacky pigs" and, swinging the little boy up in his arms, they would set off on a tour of the yard and paddock, giving me a chance to get on with some jobs unhindered.

CHAPTER TEN

In September of 1944 we had our first daughter. I was prepared this time for all that might take place, and had orders from Dear Doctor to get there as soon as I had any pains! I'd been riding a bike only a few weeks before, and continued with the daily round, feeling very fit. Lill was to live in the house to look after Tony, Jack, and the men, as father-in-law was ill from what proved to be a fatal cancer, so mother-in-law couldn't leave him for long.

Unfortunately we were in the middle of harvest, all ready to start "leading." Jack didn't expect to get to see me regularly while I was in hospital, but the weather was so bad that he valiantly cycled to Brid each evening. Petrol was still in short supply, but I was collected by car, and remember seeing Tony in the hospital doorway (children were not allowed to visit) and hearing him call excitedly: "Where's Jenmar?" We called our daughter Jennifer, but for months afterwards Tony found it a difficult word. He hadn't been carefully prepared for the birth of a brother or sister as children are today, but accepted it as a matter of course.

Again the new baby, extra small and luckily sleepy — fitted into our routine, and the only trouble was keeping Tony from upsetting the pram in his anxiety to look at her, or from throwing in such unsuitable playthings as a heavy, wooden engine. So — a sheep-bar was "rigged up" across the porch doorway, and the pram had to remain in the shelter.

Most toys were made of wood, and there was little variety in the shops. Someone made a very pretty rattle, just a little stick covered with green crochet work which formed a "stem," from which blue crochet bells hung in clusters. Inside each cluster of "petals" little brass bells were hidden, and jingled merrily when shaken. This little toy could be washed, and was used by all the family.

When we had prisoners of war to help on the farm as extra labour, they made welcome gifts. Two Italians came first, and seemed surprised that I worked so hard. They offered us a pair of slippers made from plaited binder twine. They were somewhat prickly for the feet, but "coupon free," and they also made good strong baskets from "Massey-Harris," as the twine was called, and these lasted many years.

When the "Ities" had gone, we were sent a "Jerry" prisoner called

Hermann. I admit to being rather fearful the first time we met, but he was a wonderful worker, and a very nice chap. We were all fond of him. Strange that he fitted in so well, yet the war was still raging and the Blitz continued to devastate our cities.

Hermann made the children a lovely carved wooden toy: four cockerels on a board, all nicely shaped and painted. By means of a system of strings attached to a cotton reel underneath the board, the cockerels pecked with great gusto when the toy was agitated by hand movement.

It is almost impossible now to visualise shops with so few goods on the shelves. We went to a lot of trouble to get a little wooden tractor made for Tony, and there was great excitement when Jack found someone who wanted to sell a second-hand pedal car! This was a very strong pre-war model, and needed to be, with all the hard pedalling and bashing around it got from the new owner.

When something really pretty and attractive appeared in a shop, it was quicky swooped on, and would be in the "export reject" category. One came home very thrilled to have something so beautiful for a present. We were very starved of beauty with so much "utility" ware, which was all that we in this country were allowed. Clothes were on coupons, but reasonably good quality, though they had to last a long time, with much time spent on "make do and mend."

Jack went shopping every Saturday afternoon, taking Tony in the car while I usually gave the kitchen floor a wash. There wasn't a lot of household shopping, just things like "Baccy" and the sweet ration. We took eggs to sell (Black Market) to a few friends who were very grateful. Once when I found time to go too, I missed the handle of the basket when slipping my arm through, and two dozen eggs landed on the pavement and gutter in one mighty splosh! Complete panic! Jack had visions of being arrested on the spot, so we had to hurriedly dash into the house for a bucket and water to remove the tell-tale debris!

I more often had my occasional visit to shops or the dentist by using the bus when a baby-sitter could be arranged. About this time the teenage daughter from a nearby farm often came to take the children for a walk, and, as they grew older, to tea in her home. This was a great help to me, and a treat for the little ones.

"Outings" were few and far between, but occasionally we had some legitimate reason for visiting friends and relations. If not, we were not above the ruse of putting some straw in the trailer behind the car, to look as if we were going to collect a calf or pig! On the way home, of course, we had just delivered one!

Early in 1945 Jack's father died, and the tenancy of Manor House was given up. There was a sale of stock and surplus implements, always a sad affair, and eventually mother-in-law moved to a little house in Bessingby, near Bridlington. She often came to help me, or to stay with the children, and they loved to be taken to visit her in that pretty little village.

One summer evening in that year, Jack had a lucky escape from serious injury. I was sewing, or more likely mending, in the house and so missed it all. Jack had gone into the grass field at the back of the house and had taken his sheepdog with him for a walk around the cows. One newly calved cow, known as Fat Doris, had calved the previous night (calves were taken away at birth) and when she saw the dog, her mother-instinct made her rush at it, and in doing so knocked Jack off his balance and he landed on the ground at her feet. Probably thinking he was the dog (which had dashed from her sight) she proceeded to attack him, bellowing noisily, which excited the rest of the herd to join in the fun.

By a great stroke of good fortune, Charlie at that moment decided to walk out to the shed to inspect a bicycle puncture he'd recently mended. Hearing the bellowing cows, he hurried to the field, grabbing a heavy stick on the way. The cows soon calmed down at the sight of him waving the stick, and Jack was able to roll over and over till he reached the hedge, and managed to crawl through.

He was badly shaken and bruised, and I could only thank God that Charlie had been in the right place at the right time and rescued him from what could have been a very nasty situation. Jack saw Dear Doctor the next morning, but he found nothing more serious than badly bruised ribs. We have never forgotten that evening, and have always advised people to keep dogs away when walking among newly calved cows.

CHAPTER ELEVEN

As the war ended, many restrictions ended too, though not the rationing. We were able to drive where we liked, and were free to go down to the beach for the odd half day. The concrete blocks were still there, but made good shelters from the winds and for changing into bathing things. I'd always loved swimming, and it was lovely to be able to splash around with little Tony, who wore a swimsuit cut down from an ancient woollen one, once worn by my father!

We could go to dances again, and I shall always recall the joy of getting out my 1939 blue lace Susan Small evening dress, which was bought when I still expected to return to Devon. It had been stowed away in tissue paper, and still fitted! We set off in style to a local hunt ball, Jack in his Burton label dinner jacket with a tag in a pocket stating the price of fifty-two shillings and six pence! My dress had been a great extravagance at six guineas.

We forgot, for a few hours, that we were a hard-working farming couple, and really enjoyed the enchanted evenings with a good dance band playing all the popular numbers as we swirled round the ballroom floors of the City Hall, Hull, the Spa in Brid or the Floral Hall in Hornsea. We really felt the dark days were over, and concentrated our efforts on the lively quicksteps and Paul Jones, or the more graceful waltzes and valetas.

There was some good films (known as "old movies" on TV) to see at the two cinemas in Brid or plays by the Repertory Company at the Pavilion. One evening, after rushing to finish off jobs before setting off, we arrived at the theatre where I settled back luxuriously in my soft plush seat, then unbuttoned my coat to reveal an apron over my "smart" dress! What a come-down, as one always dressed up to go to the theatre in those days. However, I soon whipped off the offending garment and stowed it in my handbag.

Meanwhile, our farm stock was increasing, and the Friesian herd doing well. In 1944 we had installed a milking machine, and the cowhouse was altered to comply with regulations for going Tuberculin Tested. There were twenty-five cows now, and they were milked three times a day. It was always difficult in winter evenings to wake up poor Jack at nine o'clock when he was so comfortable in his fireside chair to tell him it was milking time. White coats had to

Our first tractor – "Charlie."

Tractor with binder.

Elevator for stacking hay, 1946.

be worn, and they were difficult to get clean on wash-days, as well as taking a long time to dry.

We were visited once a month by the Milk Recorder, who sometimes had to be given a bed for the night! Not so easy to quickly air a feather mattress!

All this "hygiene" meant quite a lot of extra work, and the lad who lived in was surprised when he learned the meaning of "bacteria," which kept cropping up in conversation. "Oh," he said, "is that what it me-ans. Ah thort it were a fancy wod fer shit!"

We had a run of too many bull calves, which was depressing as they were worth little compared with heifers for herd replacements, and also more vet bills than usual when we had a period of mastitis, which proved difficult to eradicate.

There was still much laborious land work, and poultry was reared as another sideline. This took up much time — rearing cockerels, cleaning out huts, and "fastening up" at nights.

In February 1946 our second daughter, Marueen, was born, and both mother-in-law and Lill coped with the other two while I had my third "fortnight's holiday." Baby number three was easier to cope with, as, being wintertime, Jack had more time to help, and especially liked to put the older two to bed while I bathed and fed the newest member of the family.

It was quite difficult though, in lamplight, or carrying candles around with a baby under one arm, while keeping an eye on the toddler. We had a treasure of an oil stove, which made the bathroom warm while casting pretty patterns on the sloping ceiling. It was always known as "warmy lamp," which was Tony's word for it.

Another of his sayings about that time was often quoted in later years. "Helping" me one day to tidy our bedroom he saw a bra hanging on a chair: "Look, Mummie," he said, "this is what you keep Maureen's dinner in isn't it?"

Another milestone in our progress towards more civilised living was the arrival of telephone posts, and the installation of a phone! At last Jack felt that perhaps it would be an advantage to have one, rather than rely on driving up to the village. Once we'd got it, of course, he soon wondered however we'd managed without it!

We were especially glad to have it one night, when it was necessary to call the doctor. Our diet, in and after the war years, was deficient in many ways. Oranges, bananas, and other imported fruit were very scarce, if not unobtainable, and the flour was said to be lacking in goodness. Whatever the cause, Jack, like many others, had recurring trouble with boils, and tried various remedies, injections and prescriptions.

One, however, was particularly painful, and in spite of using some vicious ointment, grew into a very large carbuncle in the most private place! One night, after suffering agony from the application of ointment, he went to bed, but not to sleep. A blood vessel broke, sending us into a panic. I dashed down to the precious phone, and within fifteen minutes Dear Doctor's Lagonda came whizzing up the lane!

He quickly calmed us, and dealt with the emergency — but, oh dear! What a difficult area to treat, and all by candle-light, till I was sent downstairs for the big torch, which I shone on the vital part! As soon as the little operation was complete we all had a good laugh!

How lucky we were that a local G.P. could drive out to a farm to give help and confidence. Now it's all group practices, health centres, and getting the patient to surgery or hospital to be seen by total strangers.

We were especially fortunate that this doctor kept his horse with us, also a pony for his family, and often came to ride on Sundays, and at the same time would deal with a tiresome cough, give an injection, vaccination, or whatever was needed. Sundays in winter were often the only days when I had time to walk out in the fresh air.

It wasn't long before we felt our children must have a pony, and so Dante joined the family. Tony was not interested, as it was devoid of engine, brakes, and wheels. Jennifer, and later Maureen, loved to be given rides, so the first of a long, long line of almost every type of pony and horse came into our lives! After all, it was a pony which first caused me to re-visit Manor House after the Devon years!

All through the war years we had enjoyed having visitors whenever possible, and always managed somehow to put on good, if somewhat plain meals. My mother, Lill, and other "family" often came out from Brid, bringing food "treats" such as fish with them. Joan was another frequent visitor in time off from Land Army duty, and was a great help too in many ways. Helping with the children, or driving me on little excursions to places along the coast, or for a special shopping day in Hull.

Les was a childhood friend of Jack's, a bachelor with a heart of gold. He too was welcome for weekend visits, even if he found the house in winter rather cold and damp, being a chilly mortal. He was Tony's godfather, and very popular with all the children.

Mickey, Pam and Betty and Joyce all visited us as they were more free to travel after the war. Apart from Joyce, they'd married later than I did, and their families were considerably younger than ours, which in the years to come was rather nice as our little girls could "mother" their babies!

CHAPTER TWELVE

In late February 1947 we had a terrible blizzard which was unusual so near the coast. There were problems in getting the milk away, and it was taken across fields in a cart. Jack went shopping, taking neighbours too, perched in a cart behind a tractor. There weren't any snow ploughs to clear the lane, but a tumbrill (square wooden cattle trough) was trailed by tractor to make a track. I had to manage without my faithful helps in the house where we banked up the fires to keep warm.

Unknown to us, the fine, driving snow of the blizzard had blown under the pantiled roof, which was not underdrawn. The first sign we had of the trouble to follow were drips which started to seep through our bedroom ceiling!

We rolled back the carpet, moved the furniture around, and found bowls to collect the melting snow. A day later the girls' bedroom ceiling became very wet, and a piece of it dropped on the carpet, so they were moved in with Tony, who had the little room with sloping roof next to the bathroom.

We sought help, having informed the estate through Uncle J.O., and a ladder was taken up to the narrow landing where there was a small trap door which was the only access to the roof space. The men helped Jack to chuck down as much snow, bird dirt and straw as they could scrape up, but there was still a lot of melting snow which continued to cause devastation. This lasted from 28th February till 19th March, when the old diary entry reads "ceilings stopped dripping at last."

Tony's little bedroom and the bathroom were the only dry places upstairs. We moved our bed into the one dry corner of our bedroom, and covered the furniture with stack sheets. Carpets of course were all rolled up, including the stair carpet.

The spare bedroom ceiling collapsed as did the little square over the staircase. Wet patches appeared on the sitting room ceiling with a few drips, then the "men's" bedroom up the other staircase suffered too, and eventually a large chunk of plaster came down. We had no alternative than to move Charlie and his heavy old iron bed-stead into the sitting-room — complete with "po"! Luckily we had only one man living in that winter. The sitting room furniture of course had to be shifted around, the carpet rolled up like the others, and Charlie's "box" brought down to stand by his bed. Being one of the old-fashioned type he still kept his personal belongings in the traditional wooden box.

Looking back, I don't know how we survived that period. I remember thinking that we'd have to move out if things got any worse, and I felt like running away from our dripping, damp, old house. However, as there was nowhere to go, we stuck it out! It was rather like being aboard a damaged ship and wondering if we could survive the storm.

Our bedroom ceiling, contrary to all expectations, slowly tightened as it dried, and no plaster fell, yet it had had more water through it than any of the others. Men appeared to repair the ceilings, or to replace them with plaster-board, but the actual roof was not improved at all.

Mother-in-law helped to get the house back to normal and the spring cleaning that year took even longer than usual. We covered much of the water damage with "distemper," not always satisfactory, as it was inclined to rub off, and if you hadn't mixed enough to go round the whole room, the colour would vary! However, it all looked tidier, and what a relief to get the house back to normal with everyone sleeping in the right rooms again!

Each year, as a routine thing, we "whitened the tops" of the living rooms as they looked grubby after a winter of open fires, oil lamps and candles. The whitening used for the back places, including dairy walls, was bought by the stone in bags, and was messy stuff to say the least of it. No wonder we tied scarves over our heads and wore old overalls! Newspapers, as well as dustsheets, were spread over the floors to soak up the splashes.

For the "best" rooms we used a more refined powdery stuff called "white-all" which, at one shilling and sixpence per packet, was considered rather extravagant! This still splashed if used in a hurry, and I always seemed to be in a hurry, fitting in the decorating with one eye on the clock, as it was usually time to put a meal on the table, or to give the baby a feed. When they got on to more solid feeding than breast milk, I made groats, which had to be stirred, rather like making porridge, over a low heat. Later on, when vegetables were introduced, these had to be sieved as there were no cans or jars of instant baby-food.

I remember doing the sitting-room ceiling with the current baby sitting up in her pram and pushing her up and down the room while moving the steps and trying to keep her out of reach of the splashes! I was used to chatting to keep the children amused as I worked, and sometimes even stood on one leg while at the sink or kitchen table and endeavouring to keep the pram moving a little with the other foot, to save the whimpering from becoming a full-throated yell!

All bedcovers (the feather beds and woollen mattresses always had white cotton covers) had to be washed each spring and carefully ironed — even the tapes! Curtains were mostly light cotton material and were washed as each room was tackled in turn. Every drawer was pulled out, the cavity swept with a goose-wing, and the contents of the drawer tidily replaced on clean lining paper. It wasn't such a good idea to use newspaper for this purpose as it was tell-tale proof if you skipped this duty - your sins were found out the following year!

Carpets were taken up with the underfelts, folded in four, and either pushed out to the garden through a window or laboriously carried down the stairs to the front door. They were then trailed over the grass to freshen the colours. It was a help to have two people for this job, and often the carpets would then be draped over the thorn hedge till the men could help with the shaking and beating in the dinner hour. This meant having a man or woman at each corner; the men would shake with one hand, while beating with a walking stick held in the other. Then all would lift their corners in unison, causing the carpet to rise, releasing clouds of dust in the first go! We were not shamed by the dirt harboured in the carpets, as Ewbanks or a brush and pan type of sweeping could not cope with deep cleaning.

While the carpet was outside, the floorboards were scrubbed with soda, household soap and hot water. Mother-in-law liked the central floor (the outsides were stained between the skirting board and the carpet) to dry "as white as driven snow," and told me that very particular people used to rinse them with a pail of clear water to get them really clean. I couldn't see why these out-of-sight boards needed all this attention. It must have gone back to the days when household pests, "bugs" and moths in particular, were rife. As the years went by I lost this phobia for scrubbing, and a quick wash-over sufficed! Now, of course, with so many fitted carpets the floorboards never see the light of day at all!

The furniture was heavy to move around at "cleaning time" too, especially the wardrobes. We had been given a specially large one from Manor House. Beautiful quality, solid mahogany, it was made

74

in three sections which fitted into a base. The ornamental top piece was separate, and fitted over the whole length when all else was assembled. It had been bought for three pounds at a farm sale when father-in-law as a bachelor took over his first farm. People thought it would be difficult to move, not realising it all "took to pieces," but it was still a major operation to move.

Heavy double doors, one with a full-length mirror, opened to reveal three wide storage shelves which pulled out as in shop fitments; underneath the shelves was a four-height chest of drawers with polished front and brass handles which folded flat. Another heavy door hid hanging space for dresses with a deep drawer, presumably for hats! This vast area of mahogany took a long time to polish (after washing with vinegar and water), and Lill took great pride in such a job. It certainly "came up lovely" or "as bright as a bullace" as mother-in-law said — a bullace being a small, dark, wild plum.

My mother bought a reproduction hallstand, which was delivered to the house in Brid, while Lill had been helping me with our bedroom. She was an outspoken person, and, taking one look at the new piece of furniture, turned to mother and said in a scathing tone: "Fancy buying rubbish like this, I've been polishing beautiful mahogany all the afternoon!"

Ottomans were much in fashion, very useful for the storage of blankets, bed linen, or toys. We had three, and all had their uses and had originally been "men's boxes." These were joiner-made chests which all farm lads used for the storage of their belongings. They were taken from farm to farm when they "changed spots" at Martinmas. For easy handling they had a brass handle at either end, and most had a little "secret" drawer slotted under the narrow compartment partitioned off at one end. This would be used for money or a watch and other important possessions.

Another type, longer and less deep, had at one time been altered to make a home for some baby chicks which mother-in-law had in the house in a cold spring. She got a joiner to bore air holes in the lid and to make a little "pop hole" with sliding door in one end! I suppose she had a little wire run as well. Anyway, the holes and little door are still there under a pretty floral cover! I expect the story of the chicks will be handed down as family history.

We padded all the tops of such boxes with a pillow and covered them, making matching frills which were slotted on Woolworth's expanding rods. These rods seemed a wonderful improvement after cornice poles with their ugly rings — very out-of-date! All our window curtains were attached to such rods — till we could afford the metal "railway track" type. Later still came the plastic variety while the "smart" people reverted to cornice poles! The ottomans have mostly been stripped to reveal the natural wood and so look more like men's boxes again!

CHAPTER THIRTEEN

Our third daughter, Rachel, was born in November 1947 — the last fortnight's holiday as it proved, and rather to my embarrassment I found our family now consisted of "four under five"! While lying in bed after the birth I "listened in" to the wedding ceremony of the Princess Elizabeth to the Duke of Edinburgh.

Poor Jack had a difficult time while I had my enforced rest, as Jennifer, then three years old, climbed onto a propped-up gate one morning, with him in the buildings, and slipped with one leg awkwardly caught between the bars. Jack carried her carefully into the house, realising all was not well, and quickly made use of the telephone to ask Dear Doctor what he should do. He must go to the hospital and meet him there. Luckily Uncle J.O. was around and able to drive his car with Jack nursing the little girl in the back seat. Mother-in-law was in the house with Maureen and Tony.

Jennifer was X-rayed and found to have a fractured femur, and was soon in a hospital bed with both legs slung from a beam, making her little bottom clear of the mattress. Dear Doctor called specially at the Maternity Home to break the news to me. I was devastated, as I couldn't bear to think of our lively little girl having to spend six weeks in so uncomfortable a position.

However, with the knack children have in such cases, she quickly adapted to her new situation, and was spoilt by the loving attention of nurses and visitors. Jack had two patients to visit daily, and when I was allowed home I too was able to see how happy Jennifer was, swinging and twirling in all directions and surrounded by dolls and toys.

Again we were glad it was wintertime, as Jack was able to cope at bedtime. He was so good with them, and they of course loved having all his attention plus all the games in the bath, and the stories afterwards.

Christmas was difficult with a new baby, plus all the hospital visits, but we all had a festive meal with mother and others of the family in Brid, where Lill cooked turkey to perfection as she had done for as long as I could remember. Afterwards, leaving the other three, we went to the hospital to take Jennifer her presents. In spite of so many parcels the poor little girl was at the worst stage of the whole period as her legs were being let down, causing pain and discomfort. Gradually she was able to use her limbs again, and in early January we fetched her home. Luckily, the farm work wasn't too demanding, as Jack had to make time to come indoors to help me, and to teach Jennifer to walk again, as she found it easier to crawl!

With so much time spent in coping with the four little ones, we tried to cut down on work indoors. First, I stopped making bread, and then we ordered a haircord carpet for the kitchen floor! "Did you ever hear of carpet in the kitchen?" was the general reaction, but it was a boon after all that floor washing, and so much warmer underfoot and for the little ones to play around on.

Also, before long we had an electric light plant. Great excitement! The "engine" was installed in a building near the back yard and controlled by a button in the house. Of course we didn't press it in the daylight unnecessarily, but I could use the second-hand upright metal "Hoover" and the electic iron, though it was usually dark before I got round to that job. Tilly lamps were still needed in the buildings, but how much easier life seemed when the "chug chug" of the generator filled the house with light. The power wasn't strong enough for any other labour-saving gadgets, though I would have liked a little fire.

My mother bought an electric washer and took great pride in using it, and also in doing all our heavy washing too — so I really was becoming quite spoilt by such easy living! Nappies of course were still a daily chore, and I usually prepared all vegetables in the evenings. Otherwise dinner would never have been on the table at twelve! There were two men to feed as well as all of us.

The children took up a lot of time, even though Tony had become a schoolboy in the spring term. With no play-school to prepare him, he went off each morning by bus with boys from the next farm to see him on the way and hand him over to another pupil attending the same school.

The little girls amused themselves. Rachel at that time was in her pram for most of the day, and the little garden was a safe area in which to play. Of course they often only wanted to be where I was working, and I was constantly stopping to answer requests for help with a puzzle or to dress a doll. Arguments had to be settled and tantrums dealt with, and like all young mums there were days when I felt the little horrors would drive me mad.

If Jack was busy at bedtimes I enjoyed reading stories, and often chose my old favourites of "Black Beauty," "Peter Pan" and "Alice." Taken chapter by chapter they lasted quite a long time. Little memories stick in one's mind, and in the middle of a sentence about the old master in "Black Beauty" carrying his invalid "mistress" up the steps, Jennifer asked: "Was the 'mistress' his wife?" "Yes," I answered, "why?" "Because I don't think daddy would ever be able to carry you up steps! " I was on the heavy side I must admit.

One thing that Jack missed in the children's early years was the opening of stockings on Christmas morning. The first milking time of the day always coincided with this exciting ritual, so it was to me that they staggered with happy faces and bulging stockings or pillow-cases. It was never quite the same for Jack to be shown them when he came into breakfast, though from the children's point of view they had a second astonished parent to impress with the new gifts which had so mysteriously materialised overnight!

Soon after Tony started school he developed measles, but luckily not badly. Soon it was Jennifer who lay in bed with the curtains drawn, and our large old hand-bell (from Newland Park days) beside her to summon me from downstairs. When feeling a little better she lay on the couch and could take an interest in what went on.

Maureen stomped round the house, covered in spots, saying "NOT got measles" and mostly refused to even give in and be tucked up! Rachel, only six months old, was carried around to sit with me on the bed or couch while amusing the invalids, and quite surprisingly never succumbed to the infection.

It was a later illness, a particularly nasty cough, which affected them all badly and was the only time when we had really disturbed nights — so on the whole we were lucky. Perhaps the cold house had the power to kill "all known germs" as the adverts say today, or perhaps I passed on my immunity through all that breast-feeding, as I never had to buy a bottle and saved much time in that way, and money of course.

The children all loved to be taken round the farm, and the girls especially enjoyed "helping" Jack with poultry and stock. Tony was getting to the stage of helping with tractor work. They were very interested in the births of pigs, calves and lambs. Once, when having an afternoon in Brid to visit the hairdresser in town, Jennifer and

Jack gets a helping hand from his three daughters – Jennifer, Rachel and Maureen.

Maureen were playing on the floor of the cubicle. Suddenly, I heard a "Moo" and the explanation "I'm a cow, and I've just had a calf." The hairdresser, a rather staid spinster, luckily thought it very amusing!

I seldom found time to go for walks or to push the pram, but on fine, hot days would make the effort to walk down to the beach, when one might put two on the big pram and encourage the others to walk. It was worth it all to enjoy the sand and sea, and after milking time Jack would bring the car with the trailer to collect us and the pram for the return journey.

We had many visits in the summer. My school friends all came at various times with husbands and families — and all fitted in well and loved the farm life plus the nearby beach. To me it was a treat to catch up on news and talk over old times and compare domestic difficulties.

We loved to visit other Megginsons on the Wolds with children older than ours who could "mother" them, leaving us free. On these outings I looked with envy on the wide Wold landscape, the dales, the hills and the outlying farms with sheltering clumps of trees. Little did I think we would be moving to that area before many years had passed.

We were both riding again in limited spare time, as Jack had soon

Jennifer and Rachel help with the chickens.

Tony was getting to the stage of helping with tractor-work.

decided it was easier to ride with the little girls on a leading rein than to walk beside the pony. This interest in horses has remained throughout our lives, giving the greatest pleasures, and also the most sad moments. One can't be very involved with the world of horses, especially in competitive occasions, without experiencing heartbreak in one way or another.

However, in those early days the ponies gave us our recreation without travelling far. The beach was our favourite place for family rides, cantering along the golden, firm sand, with the rhythmic thudding of hooves, the wind in our faces, and the sparlking waves with their ever-changing colours. Memories we shall never forget — along to Barmston in one direction and Bridlington in the other, usually returning along the main road, using the wide grass verges.

The girls were encouraged to help in all ways, and always did their share of mucking out as they grew big enough, and cleaning "tack." While young, they also liked to "help" me with baking, though I could get on much quicker without them! Three little stools would be dragged up to the big table to enable them to reach. Some misguided person had bought all three baking boards with matching little rolling pins, and these came into action with much pounding of pieces of pastry, which took on a greyish shade before being pronounced ready to put into the little tins and then given to me to put in the oven. Oh dear, the trouble I got into if I let any of the little "pies" burn, but I'm afraid most ended in the dog's dish.

My patience was tested when clothes were covered in flour — in spite of the pinnies — and bits of pastry were trodden into the floor. Like all mums, I found that when the children were too young to really help they were always keen to do so, yet later when quite capable of tackling a job efficiently they never wanted to, and would do anything to dodge the work. There was much squabbling of the kind: "SHE'S not done it," "It's HER turn," "I helped last time," and so on!

Children's clothes were far from easy to cope with in those days. The little girls wore dresses with puffed sleeves and gathered skirts. Oh, the ironing! Cotton in the summer, Vyella in the winter. I made little aprons to play in to save having to change daily. When they went out to play in cold weather they had tweed coats with matching "pull-ups" — buttoned from knee to ankle. Poor Jack, fumbling with large hands to get them fastened. Three lots were no joke, though we thought they looked smart. I often think of them now, when small children have such easy clothes from "baby-grows" to nylon, all-in-one snow suits. We had to fasten woolly bonnets and push reluctant fingers into woolly gloves. Zip fasteners were not in general use, so dresses were all buttons, press-studs, or hooks and eyes.

We had a friend of mother-in-law who was the old-fashioned type of spinster sewing lady. She often visited houses for a week, staying as a guest on remote farms, where much mending and dress-making awaited the arrival of Miss H. She even had the job of turning sheets "sides to middles" to get more wear from the worn ones.

A gentle, quiet little person who was, I'm sure, a Godsend to many families. Because she lived near mother-in-law she did our dress-making or household sewing — if more difficult than plain curtain-making — in mother-in-law's little house, and we visited her there. What a lot of work she did for a few shillings and her "keep."

I had a great ambition for the three little girls to be dressed alike, having admired a family at school whose mother always dressed her three daughters in identical frocks. All the class used to wait with interest to see the latest creations, especially in party frocks.

Well, I only achieved these dizzy heights of elegance once. I bought three finely striped cotton dresses with smocking at yoke and waist, all the same colour, and the effect was charming! However, poor Rachel still moans about how sick she was of the sight of the wretched frocks, by the time she had worn out the one originally bought for Jennifer!

The experience was NOT repeated, though Miss H. did make velveteen corduroy "best" dresses in different colours, but, on the whole, quite naturally, the girls preferred to be individuals. Economy, however, necessitated the habit of "handing down."

There were no play-schools so, of course, the children learned to give and take among themselves, often with bouts of shrieking on my part to "sort them out." Tony was inclined to play separately, lost in his own world of making dreadful engine noises as an accompaniment.

One remembers minor incidents, visualising the children when little. One Sunday afternoon we were tidying the garden with the family playing around. A pair of steps had been left propped up against the brick wall which divided the back yard from the fold yard. Between garden and back yard there was a little gate, usually open. The fold yard was convenient for me to reach up and sling over the "pig bucket" and other household refuse (there were no dustbins, so tins and bottles went to a "tip"). As we worked in the garden we all suddenly realised that Rachel was missing! A quick look round, then seeing the steps, we peered with anxious faces over the wall, just in time to see a pathetic, unrecognisable figure staggering from the mess under the wall, where an iron-hooped pig trough was overflowing. It must have been a time when the pigs were fastened up. Thankfully, Jack grabbed the poor little soul in his arms, grateful that she hadn't hit the ironwork of the trough. Her fall had been cushioned by the revolting accumulation of tea-leaves, potato peelings and other rotting mess.

The child couldn't see, as her whole face was covered in filth, and she could only gulp in her distress. We ran the kitchen taps, and literally held her head underneath while trying to calm and reassure her at the same time. The other three gazed in awe at their little sister. Gradually the hair, complete with ribbon, was clean enough to partially dry, and then she was taken up to the bath where the cleaning process was completed!

Soon, everyone laughed, including the unfortunate victim, but we still felt it could have been a serious accident, and were careful not to leave steps propped up when not in use.

CHAPTER FOURTEEN

One autumn, when our neighbours were having a threshing day, their young son came running up the lane, white-faced and breathless, to ask me to phone for the fire brigade! Their haystack had caught fire — spontaneous combustion — and was very close to the newly formed strawstack. I quickly phoned, then ran up to the landing window where I could see the frightening flames and great clouds of smoke rising in the direction of the stackyard.

Jack had had to go to Bridlington, but on his return immediately rushed off to lend a hand, taking our two lads with him. Fire brigades were soon tearing down the lane from both Bridlington and Driffield. Water was the main worry, and our pond was soon pumped dry, so tenders had to be filled from the main road hydrants. The ever-increasing blaze was a horrifying sight, and it seemed a long time before the flames subsided, giving place to pungent black smoke which bellowed in the wind.

All that night the work of saving what was possible continued, and relays of firemen were fortified with food and drink provided by the farmer's wife and daughter. Fresh supplies of tea and provisions were fetched from Bridlington as work went on. The heart-breaking sight of a year's corn harvest being carted and then spread over nearby fields in black soggy heaps is a thing that lasts in the memory.

Jack and the men returned home at midnight, weary and red-eyed, with smoke-streaked faces. After helping all the following day again until midnight, the most urgent part of the job was over, and there was no fear of the fire starting up again. The smell of this disaster lingered for some time and cast a gloom over the neighbourhood. Of course, many folk offered straw and hay, but it was not only the financial loss, helped by insurance, but the inconvenience for many months resulting from the shortage of fodder and bedding and so much general chaos to sort out.

By this time Jack decided that we needed an extra lad to live in, to replace one who left, and so decided to try a Y.M.C.A. scheme "British Boys for British Farms." Through this we employed Philip, who settled down well considering he came from a West Riding town and had little knowledge of country life. Before he came we had a leaflet sent to us, stipulating the standard of living requested. One was "a bed to himself" — so ended the custom of expecting farm lads to share a double bed. We bought a second-hand wooden bedstead for Tony, and moved his little iron bed into the men's room for Philip. We tried to make this bare room look more cosy. The tiny window looked out on to the fold yard. "Dear Mum," we imagined him writing home, "there isn't much of a view from my bedroom and I have to lie on my belly to see it!"

We also had to provide facilities for bathing, so that was another step up in the standard of "living-in" lads. They still ate meals in the back kitchen, but sat by the front kitchen fire when at home in the evenings. We sat in the playroom with connecting door , and didn't think it at all odd that we should leave that door ajar, so the men could hear whatever wireless programme we were tuned in to! No farm worker would have thought of buying his own radio, and of course there was the problem of getting batteries for them. The men would cycle to Brid in all weathers, often three nights a week, and sometimes set off before the shops closed on Saturdays.

During the spring of 1952 I decided to attend confirmation classes. Quite a big decision at that mature age, but I began to realise that I couldn't expect any of our children to become full members of the church (which we'd rather neglected in chaotic baby-rearing years!) if Mum hadn't bothered. Also I felt the need to join Jack in being able to receive the sacrament. So — off I pedalled to private classes (being the only candidate in the parish) to Barmston on Thursday afternoons on the old bike, and have always been glad of that decision.

Eventually the confirmation date was fixed at Burton Agnes church in mid June. We arranged for mother-in-law to stay with the children that Thursday evening, and Jack would take me to the service. Well ... it was haytime, and as the afternoon wore on it became clear that in no way could he accompany me. So, for the first and last time in our years on a farm, I called a taxi! Off I went to this important occasion all alone! I did get a lift home, but this just shows that one can never plan ahead, and that farm work comes first, especially in this case of making hay while the sun shone!

I spent a lot of time working indoors, but would cycle down the fields when taking "looances" often bumping over rough ground with the bottles of tea jangling in a basket hanging from the handlebars. We would have considered thermos flasks too expensive, but nowadays "looances" can be prepared beforehand and taken by the men to eat when it suits them. Then it was mid-morning, mid-afternoon and evenings as well in haytime and harvest, when the bottles had to be ready on the dot, though the big enamel can was still used on occasions. I don't think there is any way to make tea look less appetising than to put it in a bottle!

Our little Cairn got used to hearing me filling the bottle through a funnel, and would jump about in excitement at the thought of chasing after me on the old bike.

Thinking of that bike, I once remarked to the children that I used to cycle to school on it. Maureen was a toddler, and in an accusing fashion asked: "And who was looking after us?"

I'd always enjoyed having people around, and soon the children reached the stage of asking friends for the day, which meant we met the parents too. Food was never elaborate, and I didn't spent much time in thinking up new recipes. Trifles, jellies or tinned fruit were treats, and simple everyday "nursery" puddings were popular. There were roast meals, or stew, shepherd's pie, or sausages, with often "something on toast" at tea-time. There were baked beans too, but not in the quantities present-day children like, and crisps didn't appear on the menu at all.

In the evening, we would entertain by offering a fireside supper with sandwiches, a few pastries, and a cake. We gave tea, rather than coffee, to drink, and alcohol just never appeared other than on such occasions as weddings or christenings. Our christenings were all TEA parties in any case, with the babe wearing the "ancestral" robe, newly starched and ironed to perfection!

Birthday parties became quite a regular thing, and I enjoyed organising games and usually had someone to help with serving tea. I think children must have been better mannered in those days as we never had any damage, or anyone getting out of hand and tearing round the house. They were co-operative about games, and we gave little presents. Jennifer was the only one to have a summer party, and that made it easy with games in the stackyard with pony rides always popular. Town children loved the farm, and when my old friends visited for weekends, their children were shown round by ours, who were all a little older.

We loved to visit Margery (from Devon days) and her husband and family in far-off Wiltshire. It was far off too before the motorways, and the children kept asking: "Are we there yet?" in spite of all the games we played in the car to keep them happy. Another farm with different animals and places to visit was a great excitement. Jim and Mary came with their children, and in turn ours went to stay in Liverpool, learning about city life for a change.

When Rachel was still young I dashed off by train for the christening of a godchild — Mickey's first daughter — in London. I suppose I still looked young and unsophisticated, and when the baby cried lustily during the service the vicar suggested that perhaps someone more experienced should hold her! "Good gracious," said the grandmother, "she has FOUR of her own!"

Such weekends away were rare as it took quite a lot of organising for the children to be looked after, but I occasionally had a day in York when Jack took a cow to the sale there. This was a great joy, as I really loved York whether for shopping or exploring the old streets and buildings. Little did we think it would ever become our main shopping place, with all the cultural amenities almost on our doorstep.

I first started writing — other than regular letters to family and friends — for a farming magazine when they ran a very interesting Home Section, a great part of which was written by readers. They ran competitions with titles like "Bringing up the Under-fives" or "The Farm moves in." I hurriedly dashed off an entry for the former as, having four under-fives, I felt I knew something about the subject. I was thrilled to be a prize-winner and to get the article in print with illustrations. One featured me with a baby tucked under one arm while pouring tea from a giant-sized pot.

It's surprising how many jobs could be done in this fashion! I was also seldom without a book to read in odd, snatched moments like jam-making! All that stirring, and if it set well it spoke well of the book.

Through a Farm Women's Club associated with the farm magazine, I went to several interesting meetings and met other farm wives from different parts of the county. One in particular, Elizabeth, became a great friend, also her husband and Jack got on very well — sharing farm problems — and we loved to visit each other's homes.

Joan had married a local farmer too, so they and their family were able to continue our close contacts. When farmers get together they are never short of conversation!

In 1948, part of the estate, including Kingsfield, came up for sale. This caused us great consternation, as we felt we could never afford the asking price of £4,000. This now seems ludicrous, but we missed the opportunity, and from that time on were unsettled.

We looked at a dozen or more farms which were advertised to let, but we learned, if nothing else, that there were some far worse places than ours — very isolated, partly dilapidated, or approached by the roughest tracks imaginable. The demand for rented farms was increasing, with more favourable profits, and it was obvious that the big landlords would never have difficulties in keeping their farms tenanted as in pre-war years, when rents were waived rather than having to work the land themselves.

By 1951, after much discussion, a change in farming policy took place, and Jack made up his mind to part with his precious Friesians. This was the outcome of difficulties in finding another farm, and if there was no need to consider the suitability of buildings for a T.T. herd, it was felt there would be a wider choice.

A dispersal sale was planned for August in York, and Messrs. Hobson compiled a catalogue. Much preparation was needed, and took up a great deal of time that summer. All cows and calves had to be taught to lead well, and nearer the day all had to be spruced up and given attention to ensure that they looked their best.

The whole herd was taken by a cattle lorry the day before the sale to a special train waiting at Carnaby Station. Three men travelled with them, and, to his great joy, Tony was included in this expedition. He felt very grown-up to be "helping," and in being allowed to "sleep rough" in the market.

We went by car to see them arrive in York where they were transported from station to market. The next day we anxiously watched the sale, which was very satisfactory, but a great wrench to all who had cared for and milked those animals. They had been part of our lives, and the empty cowhouse and pasture left us with a feeling of great loss.

We bought a Jersey cow for the house, and I made butter. The separator was in use again, and we had the luxury of cream with fruit pies. I used a wooden churn for butter-making, and it had "paddles" inside. A very minute affair compared with the "end over end" variety which mother-in-law had used in her Wold farming days. I enjoyed patting our butter into neat yellow bars with patterns made by the imprint of the "Scotch hands."

CHAPTER FIFTEEN

About this time we heard of a combine harvester being used on a farm near Beeford. Jack and Uncle J.O. went to see this wonderful machine in action, but the verdict was that it would never "take on" in this country where weather is unpredictable. However, by the harvest of 1953 a contractor combined a field of barley for us. It seemed a marvellous invention, and the corn was delivered to the merchant in Bridlington the following day. Most of the harvest work went on in the traditional way, and I was still called on to lend a hand with "picking" on the stack.

During the early fifties, although still unsettled and occasionally looking at farms if any were advertised, things were gradually improving in the house, and we were getting about more. We bought a rolltop desk to accommodate the ever-increasing "office" papers and records which were overflowing from various drawers and cupboards. It's interesting to think that before the war farmers didn't have audited accounts for income tax! The desk was cumbersome and difficult to polish, but held an amazing amount of papers, files and record books.

We also bought a brand new three-piece suite. At a cost of £112, this was in the luxury class. With "Wade" upholstery in cut moquette, it replaced the older chesterfield suite which had become quite a wreck, with springs shooting out in all directions and the covers wearing very thin. So we had a funeral-pyre and watched the poor moth-ridden furniture going up in smoke. Actually, the new suite has given good service too, as it is still in use, without covers, after almost forty years.

We took the girls to dancing classes, and even attended some adult ones ourselves to brush up our ballroom style. Hunt balls and farmers' union dances were quite frequent affairs which we greatly enjoyed. Buying a new evening dress was always exciting, and my mother gave me a moleskin cape which must have added years to my appearance, but I felt most elegant when wearing it!

There was a roller-skating rink in Bridlington and the children enjoyed that while we also "had a go" at "over 20" classes in the evenings with much laughter and many bumps. Each January we took the family to a matinee of the touring company pantomime. This was a great excitement, and we wore "best" clothes while joining in all the fun of shouting back to the comedian and "singing" the words of the big song sheet, yet not sufficiently brave as to go on to the stage as some children did.

It wasn't long before mother bought a television set, and we would stay for tea after Saturday shopping to see the children's programmes. Mother and Lill were to become quite obsessed with the early television shows, and I would get phone-calls to tell me of the marvels of the previous night's viewing!

In the summer months we played tennis, as Joan and her husband had made a court, and I even cycled to Brid to play on a public court with a friend. We had a weekend most years with Margery and her farming husband in Wiltshire, and one Whitsuntide we stayed in a farm guest-house in the Lake District. That was a never-to-be-forgotten weekend with the children seeing mountains and lakes for the first time, and the pretty horned sheep with woolly, long-tailed lambs. We drove over the hard knoll pass in our long-bonneted old Humber Snipe, with hearts in our mouths, and the weather was so unexpectedly hot that the children "bathed" in mountain streams just wearing their pants.

We still spent most of our free time with horses and ponies, and quite often managed a day's hunting now all the family were at school. It meant a lot of preparation the night before, and much work before leaving to hack to the meet — sometimes as far off as Kilham or Dunnington — and returning very tired with the tea to get ready, when the inclination was to soak in a hot bath, but all well worth the effort! I was never a good rider, but my dear old skewbald cob Flicka looked after me, and I loved riding across the countryside and meeting friendly people.

This was the heyday of local shows which had just got going after the war, with many of the smaller ones sadly to fold up later on, due to the ever-rising costs. We had many happy family outings to shows around the district, sometimes taking the pony for either the "leading rein" or fancy-dress class. We had our little troubles of course — arriving too late and missing the class, or the pony proving too much of a handful for its rider, or torrential rain descending on a ballet-costumed circus star! Sometimes tempers were frayed by long waits for a class as they got more and more behind scheduled time, but some days everything went well, and we came home with rosettes and everyone in good spirits.

The first great stars of show-jumping were then at the top of this

The author with "Flicka," the well-loved pony, setting out for the beach in the old milk float with family and friends.

sport, and at the larger shows appeared in the flesh: Colonel Llewellyn, Pat Smythe, Wilf White, and many others who brought a new sport into the public eye.

At long last we knew the luxury of not having any "men" living in the house and to cook for, other than the "looances." We could now dispense with the back kitchen table, and when sitting in the evening could close the playroom door. In 1955 we actually bought a television set — black and white, of course, and one channel! Rather sadly we used the "wireless" less, played fewer games with the children, but still read a lot and encouraged them to do the same.

The "men's" bedroom became a room for Tony's train-set with which he played for hours on end, often having school friends to join him. The girls had friends who liked the farm and having rides. The skewbald cob Flicka also went in harness and I drove her in the old farm "float." Piling in the children, plus a friend or two, we would jog down to Auburn, tie up Flicka at the farm there and have a paddle or a swim, then games on the beach before driving back. Occasionally I drove into Brid and we called on grandma for a brief visit.

We also all had bikes and would sometimes go out on these, but the ponies were more popular. Occasionally, I dashed off by train to keep in touch with school friends, while Jack and mother-in-law coped with the family. After a few days in a city, be it Manchester, Liverpool, or London, I was glad to get bck to the country and the family, while feeling rested and refreshed by the change.

We were rearing Thornbers poultry and selling eggs on contract, and that meant extra work in the way of egg-washing each evening. There was also the worry of rearing young birds who had a nasty habit of smothering in their huts at night, before learning how to perch. This poultry enterprise was a help to us while living without the monthly milk cheque.

CHAPTER SIXTEEN

In 1956 we were told of a farm to let on a big estate, high up on the Wolds. We might, we were told, have a chance on recommendation. We had a few days in which to think over this idea. At first we thought it wouldn't do at all! Chiefly because of the children, now at good, easily accessible schools in Brid. We should miss our families who had given us so much help, and we felt they in their way would miss us. If we moved to the Wolds we would be "miles from anywhere." We talked of all the problems without letting anyone other than close family know of the idea.

Then, one night that week — it was mid January — the weather suddenly changed, and we had a raging blizzard, then heavy rain, with high winds.

When we went up to bed our ceiling was dripping and Jack had to go outside in the Arctic weather to fetch a stacksheet to cover up the furniture. He struggled up the stairs with his cumbersome load, and as he dumped it on the floor where I'd rolled back the carpet, he said with great feeling: "This is all we need! If we have a chance of that Wold farm we are going. I've had enough of this lark."

So, we had interviews and were inspected, then followed a long waiting period when we had little idea of where we stood until, in mid February, we heard the good news that we had been offered the new farm!

So — once more after fourteen years we were preparing for another move. This time it was a much bigger upheaval with all those years of steady accumulation of stock, implements, possessions of all kinds, to say nothing of four children!

As we went to look round the new farmhouse, which seemed like a palace in comparison to our low, damp, old home which we had tried so hard to make the best of, but it had needed constant redecorating and was so inconvenient that we had no regrets about leaving it.

The new house was large, with very high ceilings, and had been well built in 1878; it had lovely woodwork with deep skirtings and good ceilings with pretty mouldings in the main rooms. The previous tenants had had the house divided to make a farm worker's cottage in the kitchen-end, and our man, George, recently married, agreed to move with us.

"Cot Nab," our new home on the Yorkshire Wolds.

I was, of course, "over the moon" to think I would have not only "mains" electricity, but TWO proper toilets! The windows were tall, with a great expanse of sky and Wold views, and some rooms had two, including the kitchen. So much light — quite the opposite impression from the "pit pony" feeling when first seeing Kingsfield. But, oh dear, what a lot of curtain material, but mother-in-law got busy with the old sewing machine.

Gradually over the weeks before April 6th, many journeys took place along the roads (twenty-eight miles) between the coastal fam and the high Wold area. Implements behind tractors, huts on trailers, and loads of small tools, sheep bars, troughs and stakes. Corn was sown in the new fields, doubling our previous acreage, and hay, "wuzzles" and fertiliser taken to store in readiness for the move.

In the house, mother-in-law rallied round, and carpets were taken up, floors and cupboards scrubbed out, and packing cases filled. I repainted all the grocery tins to match the colour scheme of the new kitchen — we wouldn't have thought of buying storage jars — and our big cupboard and dresser also changed colour! With so much needed "outside" we had to go easy on household spending, but we did have the luxury of a brand-new carpet square for the dining-room. Good quality Axminster — it cost forty pounds.

At last the great day dawned. Jack and I went with the big old car well laden, on the evening of April 5th. The former tenants had moved out, leaving a lovely fire in the big, bare kitchen. We unloaded the sheepdog, the goldfish and the budgie in its cage. The only place we could find for that was to hang it on a bacon hook! We put a rug on the brick floor, and a coffee table, and fixed a folding bed, making ourselves comfortable for the night with — joy of joys — our electric kettle which could now be put into use. The cooker, rented from the G.E.C., was waiting to be used. Things WERE looking up!

On waking the next morning, we soon realised that we were now living on the Wolds, for a most un-springlike scene faced us as we gazed out of those high windows — snow! There it was, a fairyland of tall larch trees in the shelter belt with the morning sun shining through them to bathe the dale sides in a rose-coloured glow. I never tired of that view, though I must admit that often in winter the mist blotted it out for days on end!

However, on that first morning we had little time to admire the view. I was soon cleaning things, while Jack went back for more loads of goods and chattels and brought the children and dogs, all very excited. The sprinkling of snow soon melted, and they ran round exploring, while longing for the removal men to arrive. This time we had two large vans, and mother-in-law stayed to see the last one leave before shutting the door of Kingsfield for the last time.

Cattle lorries brought the stock, and we were all kept busy as the furniture arrived, carpets were laid, and, with the help of sister-in-law and others, we just kept on and on until the last goods were unloaded about 8 p.m. The men came into the house towards the end with assorted armfuls of teddies, dolls, a horse on wheels, and a couple of home-made hobby horses. The drawers with all puzzles and games carefully boxed had been turned on their end and everything mixed up, which took weeks to sort in the children's quiet moments. They loved tearing up and down with our large collection of books, and before night had them on the shelves.

We felt "at home" straight away, and even had the stair carpets down, as we had bought those with some of the curtains from our predecessors. How opulent we felt to have what seemed like acres of plain, green fitted carpet on stairs and long landing. It was a very

The author with snow almost as high as the five-barred gate at "Cot Nab."

exhausting day, but a happy one with many helpers and lots of "looances." By evening, mother, sister and Lill all came to look round and were suitably impressed.

The only sadness was the disappearance of a favourite cat who had refused to be caught and ran off, never to be seen again. Jack went back to try and find her, but hadn't any luck. Sukie had been a favourite puss, and we were sad to have lost her.

There was only one room in desperate need of decoration, and mother-in-law was soon busy with that. Gradually she taught me to tackle the papering, and I was able to take over that much. Although our rooms were now high and large, needing many rolls of paper, at least they were dry and the decorating lasted. We were very thrilled to be all electric, with washing-machine, fire and immersion heater. It was several years before we bought a fridge, but the dairy was cold, and there were plenty of vans to deliver our food.

We found we had very friendly neighbours, most of them within our age-group, so that there were families for our children to play with. Our lovely village nestled under the Wold, and a pretty lane led down to a grass field which was part of our farm. With a steep hillside, tall trees, a stream and primroses, it seemed like heaven. The "dale" too, although very poor pasture, was a wonderful place for riding through, and the ponies got fit on the steep slopes after the flat fields on the low-lying land they'd known on our last farm. Tony was happy as he had a surplus unwanted dairy for his train set, and this for many years was known as "the train room."

The children ran down to the village school, but plodded slowly uphill at tea-time! Bikes were not so much in use as it often meant dismounting to push the things. We soon explored the new countryside on horseback, delighting in the wonderful views and hidden tracks through remote dales. Jack did his shepherding jobs with the aid of a surefooted horse. The girls were very good assistant shepherds, and Tony a very competent tractor-driver.

We now milked Ayrshires, had several sows, about a hundred ewes, and the poultry. It was then considered safer to have some variety in stock, rather than to specialise. We were fairly well-off for labour, and though we both worked hard and long hours, we were very happy in our work. Our hearts were set on improving the farm, the house and the garden, but we could usually find time to ride with the girls or meet neighbours, and to have old friends to stay. Those

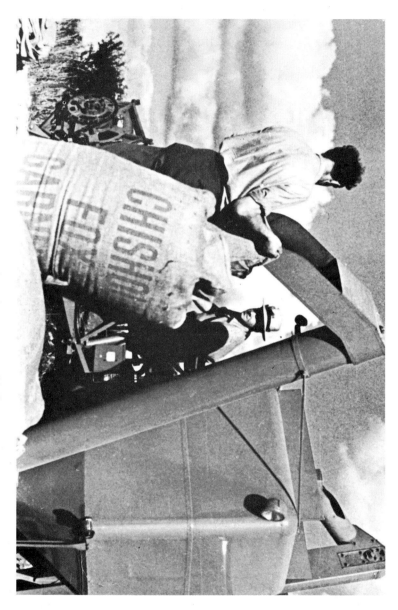

Our first combine harvester in 1962.

100

loyal people could now forget the insanitary arrangements they had endured so long at Kingsfield and could now indulge in as many baths as they wished, and go to the loo in comfort!

We were near to York, of course, and nearer to Jack's childhood friend Tom, who with his wife Vera lived on the edge of the Dales. They introduced us to that glorious part of Yorkshire when we could spare the time for weekend visits.

Jack discovered that he enjoyed building little walls in the garden, and we made a tennis court which gave much pleasure to the growing family and to friends. York was, and still is, greatly appreciated as a beautiful city to visit for shopping expeditions, with all its wonders of beautiful buildings, museums and the theatre.

The Moors and Dales were within easy distance for the odd day out, and we could still easily visit the coast and our family there. We were very much nearer to our old friend Les and to Megginson relations now that we were up on the Wolds.

The first harvest still saw the old binder clattering behind the Fordson Major, but we also had a combine! A "bagger" type, but a great innovation, and we were very proud of it. We grew oats in those days and they were still stooked, and I even helped on the stack for an odd hour. One extra wet harvest saw rotting stooks which had to be dumped into a pit, and after that the old binder went out of use. So ended an era which had begun for me as a town schoolgirl fascinated by the binding of sheaves, the stooks, and a yard full of tidy stacks.

On the credit side we'd seen the last of the threshing machine except for special displays at country fairs to show the younger folk what strange methods were used in pre-combine harvester days!

We grew seed potatoes, a new crop to us, but the altitude was suitable for the recently-formed Wold Seed Potato Growers Association. Our equipment was primitive at first, and the spuds were stored out of doors in "pies," but it was the beginning of an important crop for high Wold farms.

This change of farms was another milestone in our lives, and despite all the ups and downs, plus troubles both financial and domestic, we have, throughout the years, been contented with our life. Jack felt he had returned home to the Wolds where his life began, and where his forebears had farmed for 150 years. I, who always felt uplifted to see hills, was now surrounded by them, and loved our chalky hillside in all seasons, whatever the weather.

CHAPTER SEVENTEEN

1987

The years have rolled on at an alarming rate as we look back to the beginning of our lives. It's true that we are now old in years, but, I trust, young in spirit. Although semi-retired and living in the village, we are, thankfully, fit and well.

With Tony in charge of the farming and living "on the tops" — as we say down here — with his wife and family, Jack still goes up daily to see to the cattle. The sheep were sold when the labourious tasks of net setting and lambing times became too hard. Cows, pigs and poultry disappeared a long time ago. Milk comes in bottles, and eggs in little cartons.

Everything now is specialised, and I've taken badly to some of the changes, feeling that much of the romance has disappeared from the farming scene. One can't call a halt to progress, but only the young or mechanically minded can appreciate the elaborate machinery, the factory-like "set up" for drying corn and storing it. The vast potato sheds with pallets so easily moved by a fork-lift truck. The giant-sized round bales, the ever-changing methods to save labour, and the soaring costs of fertilisers and sprays — one sometimes wonders where it will end, and whether over-production will result in disaster.

The gangs of men who hoed, who carted "tonnips," who spent weeks "luking" and scruffling, will never be seen again. Our grandchildren have never known the fun of playing around the haycocks, or in a field of stooked corn, or the excitement as the binder finished cutting the last piece of corn when men with dogs and sticks were waiting for the poor rabbits. What would the "animal rights" people say to THAT sport!

The children of today have never known the feel of a Clydesdale's broad back as, with legs stretched astride the wide old saddle, one swayed blissfully between rows of stooks as the wagon was loaded high with golden sheaves.

The men may have worked long hours for small wages, but there was a good spirit among them, a pride in work, a "pulling together" and, above all, companionship. The latter is sadly lacking today when much work is done in solitary state — comfortable, yes, in

102

heated tractor cabs, but the conversation is one-sided as the transistor or cassettes belt out the latest pop music, or the world news.

In the farmhouse labour-saving gadgets have done away with the drudgery. The fridge and freezer are well stocked, and no vans call at the door. Everything is geared to "easy care," "non-iron" and "ready to serve."

Cooking has become sophisticated, with continental influences. It's all taken for granted, and I, too, am glad that domestic chores are light, but I feel thankful in some ways to have known the old ways. Otherwise how could one really appreciate the new?